EATING
VEGAN

EATING VEGAN

A Plant-Based Cookbook
for Beginners

DIANNE WENZ
Photography by Elysa Weitala

ROCKRIDGE
PRESS

Interior and Cover Designer: Peatra Jariya
Art Producer: Meg Baggott
Editor: Reina Glenn
Production Manager: Martin Worthington
Production Editor: Matthew Burnett

Photography © 2020 Elysa Weitala. Food styling by Victoria Woollard

Author photograph by Dennis Mason.

ISBN: Print 978-1-64611-754-3 | eBook 978-1-64611-755-0

For everyone
who wants to go vegan but
isn't sure where to start.

CONTENTS

INTRODUCTION

I went vegetarian in 1993—and it was a bit of a rocky road. While growing up, dinner usually consisted of a chicken patty with Rice-A-Roni and canned vegetables, so when I started to cook for myself, I wasn't sure how to put a healthy meal together—let alone a meatless one. I ate *a lot* of pasta and portobello mushrooms in those early days. In 2001 I went vegan, but although *I'd* learned a ton in my years of veg life, other people still didn't really understand what veganism was. I remember one lunchtime work function where the "vegan" options I had were tuna fish and egg salad (face palm). I ended up eating a pile of lettuce, contributing to the cliché that vegans only eat bunny food.

So much has changed since then and veganism is now mainstream. But I've found that newbies are still as confused as I was all those years ago. Sure, it's easy to go out and order a veggie burger, but how do you put a plant-based meal together at home? And what do you do with all those "weird" ingredients? What the heck is tempeh? How do you pronounce *quinoa*? (It's *keen*-waa.) Do I *have* to eat nutritional yeast? (Of course you don't have to eat it, but I'm willing to bet that, pretty soon, you'll be looking for excuses to do just that.)

I became a vegan health and lifestyle coach so I could guide people through the transition to this new way of living, and I became a plant-based chef to teach them how to cook the delicious meals that would help them do it. I wrote this book so I could reach more people in less time. It's kind of like the CliffsNotes version of working with me.

Eating Vegan is for new vegans and plant-curious eaters across the omnivore spectrum. It will show you what plant-based cooking is really like and give you the tools to make delicious vegan meals at home. I share some of my favorite easy recipes, along with tips and tricks to help make eating meatless easier. Most dishes here are veganized versions of old favorites—I promise, there's familiarity even with this brand-new way of eating! And you have my word that none of it will resemble bunny food. This is the book I wish I'd had all those years ago.

CHAPTER 1

VEGAN EATING 101

Congratulations for pursuing your vegan curiosity! Whether you've decided to start eating vegan out of compassion, concern for the environment, or for your health, I'm here to help. Maybe you're just hoping to add more meatless meals to your diet. That's great news, because I have lots of mouth-watering recipes for you to choose from. There's no wrong way to do it—go vegan overnight or ease into it slowly. No matter what brought you here or how you plan to approach vegan eating, you'll find plenty of information to assist you on your journey.

Consider this chapter your crash course on veganism. I'll define veganism, share reasons to eliminate animal products, and debunk myths along the way. If you've already done some reading on veganism, you may be familiar with the information I present in this chapter, so use it as a refresher. If you're a newbie, think of this as your cheat sheet.

WHAT BEING VEGAN MEANS TODAY

Once, while sitting in a quiet vegan café, I overheard the couple next to me trying to figure out the difference between "vegan" and "organic." It was a great example of how the word "vegan" tends to be misused, so I figured I'd start by setting the record straight.

Veganism is a lifestyle, not just a diet. Vegans don't eat anything that comes from an animal, including meat, eggs, milk, cheese, or honey. They also avoid using everyday products made from animals—which means they don't wear leather, silk, wool, or down—and they don't use personal care or household items that have been tested on animals.

The term "plant based" is sometimes used synonymously with the word "vegan" these days, but "plant based" can have a few meanings. A plant-based eater might be someone who follows a vegan diet but isn't on board with the lifestyle exclusions yet, or someone who has mostly transitioned to a vegan diet but occasionally eats a few eggs or a piece of meat. Sometimes people use the phrase "plant based" because they want to separate themselves from the old stereotype of vegan animal rights activists who stand outside department stores throwing red paint on rich people in fur coats. When I use the phrase "plant based" in this book, I'm talking about food: someone who eats a diet based exclusively on plants.

REASONS TO EAT A PLANT-BASED DIET

There are many reasons to eliminate animal products from your diet. Some people adopt a plant-based diet for one reason and stick with it for others. I went vegan for the animals and immediately noticed improvements in my health. Here are some of the biggest reasons people make the switch to a vegan diet.

Animal rights: Countless documentaries have depicted the deplorable living conditions of livestock in the United States. Little or no access to sunlight and cages so small the animals can't even turn around—this is the norm for pigs, cows, and chickens across the country. Many people feel helpless when they discover the meat they buy at the grocery store comes from animals that have been treated this way. Although they can't shut down the farms themselves, they can choose not to purchase their products.

Environmentalism: Animal agriculture is one of the leading causes of destruction to the planet, and it's really taking its toll on this big blue marble we call home. In fact, it's responsible for between 14.5 and 18 percent of all greenhouse gas emissions, which is more than the combined exhaust from cars, trucks, and trains. Think about it: All those animals in factory farms need to be fed, given water, and housed, and we're using the Earth's resources to do so. The waste run-off from factory farms is contaminating our water supply as well as our food. Factory farm waste has been known to pollute vegetable crops, which then leads to nationwide recalls.

Health benefits: There have been so many studies that show the health benefits of eliminating meat, dairy, and eggs from our diet. Plant-based foods don't contain any of the saturated fat or cholesterol that animal products do—instead, they're loaded with vitamins, minerals, antioxidants, phytonutrients, and fiber. The nutrients in vegetables, fruit, nuts and legumes, and whole grains can reduce inflammation in the body, which in turn reduces the risk of developing chronic diseases. Plant-based diets are known to reduce the risk of heart disease, certain cancers, type 2 diabetes, liver disease, and kidney disease.

DEBUNKING MYTHS ABOUT VEGAN LIFE

There's this old joke that goes, "How can you tell if someone is vegan? Don't worry, they'll tell you." (Eye roll.) Yes, we do sometimes tell others we're vegan, but it usually happens right after someone offers us a cheeseburger or a bacon-wrapped hot dog. We don't typically go around shouting that we're vegan to anyone who will listen. I've actually found our friends and family will announce our veganism to others. Some other vegan myths include:

Vegans are preachy. I've had friends try to hide the fact they're eating non-vegan food from me because they're afraid I'm going to judge them or start preaching about why they shouldn't eat it. It's common to believe that vegans like to police what others eat or shove their ideas down the throats of others. Okay, a lot of new vegans *do* tend to go through, what I like to call, an "overenthusiastic period" in the beginning, but once the honeymoon is over, most of us like to quietly go about our business. I have had plenty of omnivores get preachy with me after finding out I'm vegan, though, and I can't tell you how many times someone has commented "bacon" on a vegan Facebook post. Though often tempted, I've never once left a "kale" comment in retaliation.

Vegans are weak. We live in a protein-centered society, and many people (wrongly) believe meat is necessary to get adequate amounts of protein and iron. Because we don't eat meat, vegans must all be 100-pound weaklings who need to shove fistfuls of vitamins down their throats just to be able to get through the day, right? In fact, there's an abundance of nutrients in plant foods, including protein and iron, and most people actually notice an increase in energy and strength once they go vegan. Many athletes are vegan—and some of them are even record holders.

If it's vegan, it's healthy. I once gave someone a vegan cupcake and she asked how something so sinful could be so good for you. I felt bad breaking the news that I made it with white flour, two kinds of sugar, and vegetable shortening. Although whole plant foods are really good for you, there are plenty of processed vegan foods that aren't. Sure, they don't contain meat or dairy products, but they do contain lots of sugar and fat. Most sodas are technically vegan, but guzzling bottles of cola isn't going to do your body any favors, and neither will pounding down the veggie burgers and fries.

Vegans eat nothing but salad. When Lisa on *The Simpsons* went vegetarian, Homer and Bart danced around singing, "You don't win friends with salad! You don't win friends with salad!" Okay, I do kind of fit this cliché, because I love a good salad, but I top mine with hearty, filling ingredients—like roasted veggies, beans, and grains—so I'm pretty sure I *could* win a friend or two with salad. But I also really love mac and cheese, lasagna, tacos, burritos, and pizza—all free from meat and dairy products, of course. If you don't believe me, keep reading, because this cookbook contains 75 vegan recipes, and only six are salads!

WHAT TO EXPECT

Consider this book an introduction to veganism, with me as your guide to help you through this new way of eating. As this is a cookbook, I focus on the dietary side of veganism rather than the lifestyle aspect of it. In using this book, you'll be able to navigate your way around a plant-based kitchen, as well as cook quick and easy meals even picky eaters will love.

WHAT YOU'LL FIND HERE

If you're reading this book, vegan foods are probably new to you, so I'll be sharing all the information you'll need to start cooking with ingredients such as tofu, tempeh, and seitan as well as beans, whole grains, and, of course, vegetables. I'll give you tips to help improve your cooking skills plus advice on transitioning to a vegan diet. Of course, you'll find easy and delicious plant-based recipes, **none of which will take longer than 1 hour from start to finish.** Be sure to check the Resources section at the back of the book (page 146) for a list of other useful books, documentaries, websites, and apps that can help you on your vegan journey.

LABELS YOU'LL SEE IN THE RECIPES

30 Minutes or Less: These recipes take no more than 30 minutes to prepare from start to finish, including cooking time.

Gluten-free

Leftover-friendly: These recipes hold up in the refrigerator or freezer and reheat well (if needed).

Nut-free

Plan ahead: These recipes use ingredients that need to be prepped in advance (but don't worry, I'll give you an option for a store-bought substitution).

WHAT YOU WON'T FIND HERE

I'm not a member of the vegan police—I'm not here to judge you or cause guilt. I won't make any presumptions about your dietary journey and I won't break down your door to knock the food out of your hand if you decide to eat a piece of cheese. I also won't ask you to spend your life savings going vegan. I, too, like to save money at the grocery store, so I don't cook with expensive or processed ingredients. And although I love to cook, I don't want to spend all day in the kitchen, so you won't find complicated recipes, long lists of ingredients, or meals that take hours to make.

CHAPTER 2

GETTING INTO THE KITCHEN

In this chapter, you'll get to know a few new-to-you foods you'll incorporate into your diet as you experiment with vegan cooking. I recommend that you enjoy these foods for their own flavors rather than try to compare them to non-vegan counterparts. If someone tells you tofu "tastes just like chicken," they're fibbing. Tofu tastes like tofu, and soon you'll be able to cook it to your liking.

Some of these ingredients might require new cooking techniques, but I promise you they will be simple, and I'm here to help. There's always a learning curve when trying anything new. Before you know it, you'll be a pro at cooking lentils and quinoa.

The kitchen is my favorite room in the house, so let's dive in!

VEGAN STAPLES

There are a few often-used ingredients in plant-based eating that I recommend having on hand at all times. Some are typically the star of the meal, like tempeh or seitan, whereas others add flavor and texture. They may be new to non-vegans, so I'll walk you through them.

COCONUT MILK

Unlike nut milks, which are made by blending nuts and water, coconut milk comes right from the source—the coconut. It's rich and creamy and gives a lush, velvety texture to soups, curries, and sauces. When recipes call for coconut milk, look for the canned type, not the coconut milk beverage that comes in box-like packages. Give the can a good shake, because the cream and liquid can separate while sitting on the shelf.

TOFU

Many people see those white blocks of tofu at the grocery store and have no idea what they are or what to do with them. Tofu—also known as bean curd—is a springy-textured block made with soy milk, first developed in China around 2,000 years ago. It has myriad uses—scrambled for breakfast, baked and tossed into salads, mashed and turned into "cheese," blended into savory dips, the list goes on. You can usually find tofu in the produce area or refrigerator section of the grocery store. Tofu is a great source of plant-based protein in a vegan diet and is versatile to work with in that it absorbs the flavors of whatever you're cooking with it.

NUTRITIONAL YEAST

What experienced vegans refer to affectionately as "nooch," nutritional yeast is deactivated yeast that has a nutty, cheesy taste. It contains protein, vitamins, and minerals, and is a good source of vitamin B_{12}. It gives dishes a slight cheesy flavor—essential for vegan mac and cheese, and is great sprinkled on popcorn, pasta, and soups. Many vegans (myself included!) find it highly addictive and will pour it over just about everything. Find it either in the baking aisle or with the vitamins and supplements.

MISO PASTE

We probably all know miso from that soup that's served in Japanese restaurants. Miso soup is made from miso paste, which adds flavor to sauces, dips, and glazes. It's

BE CHOOSY WITH YOUR TOFU

There are a few different types of tofu and each has its own purpose.

Firm and extra-firm tofu usually come in refrigerated, water-packed tubs and need to be pressed before cooking (see page 15). They're both great for stir-fries, salads, tofu scrambles, and much more. Freezing gives these types of tofu a meaty texture, making them easy to crumble into chilis and pasta sauces.

Super firm tofu is, well . . . super firm. It has less water than firm and extra-firm tofu and is good to use right out of the package. It's great to marinate and grill or bake, and it holds up well in sandwiches.

Silken tofu comes in both refrigerated, water-packed tubs and shelf-stable packages. It's soft and kind of gelatinous, so I don't recommend eating it straight from the package. It works well blended into smoothies, dips, and puddings.

Baked tofu has already been marinated and baked, which makes it firmer and chewier. If you're pressed for time, it's a great shortcut when making salads or sandwiches.

usually made from fermented soybeans, but I have seen chickpea miso at the grocery store, too. Miso comes in several colors; typically the darker the color, the stronger and saltier the flavor. Two of the most common types of miso are red miso and mellow white miso. I like using the mellow white variety for its subtle flavor. It's usually in the refrigerated section of the grocery store, near the tofu and tempeh.

TEMPEH

Native to Indonesia, tempeh is a cake made from fermented soybeans. It's definitely an acquired taste—some people have told me it's a little too fermented for their liking. To get rid of that fermented flavor, you can steam your tempeh for a few minutes before adding it to your recipe. Simmering tempeh in a bath of warm water or broth will help remove the fermented taste, as well. It's great in stir-fries or crumbled in chilis and tacos. It's usually next to the tofu in the grocery store.

SEITAN

Seitan is 100 percent wheat gluten, so it's not for those who are sensitive to gluten. But it *is* a good source of protein. It looks a little like a slab of meat and has a very meaty texture, so it can replace meat in just about any non-vegan recipe. Slice it and add it to sandwiches, simmer it in stews, or grind it and stuff it into taco shells. Like tempeh, it's usually found near the tofu in the produce area or refrigerator section of the grocery store. It's also easy to make your own (see page 144).

WILL YOU NEED NEW APPLIANCES?

Someone once told me they couldn't go vegan because they couldn't afford to buy fancy new kitchen appliances. I will admit that I love kitchen gadgets—I have a high-speed blender and a (sadly neglected) dehydrator—but they are definitely not necessary to cook vegan food. You'll need all the same things you would for any other type of cooking, such as a cutting board, a sharp knife, pots and pans, baking dishes, and a blender. There are a few appliances that do make cooking easier, but *they're not required.*

Food processor: There's so much you can do with a food processor: chop veggies, blend sauces, mix doughs, and more. Some food processors come with attachments that make it easy to thinly slice and grate vegetables, too.

Immersion blender: These handheld blenders can blend soups and sauces right in the pot, so you don't have to wait for them to cool and pour them into a standing blender. They're also lighter and easier to store.

High-speed blender: High-speed blenders are pretty pricy, but I've found they're well worth the money. They can blend sauces and smoothies in a matter of seconds. They also make it super easy to blend raw nuts into smooth, creamy sauces with less soaking time.

Kitchen scale: A small, inexpensive digital scale will make measuring more precise. You also won't have to use (and then wash) measuring cups.

RAW NUTS

Raw nuts, cashews especially, are pretty magical—when blended with water, they become creamy sauces and cheeses. Most raw nuts aren't actually raw—they usually need to go through some sort of heat process to get them out of their shells. What you really want are nuts that haven't been roasted or salted. Because they contain oils that can go rancid, store raw nuts in your refrigerator.

CHIA SEEDS AND FLAXSEED

Chia seeds and flaxseed are both tiny nutrient powerhouses, packed with fiber, protein, omega-3 fatty acids, and calcium, among other things. They're great to throw into your smoothies or oatmeal. They turn to gel when mixed with water and can even take the place of eggs in baking. They can be a little tricky to find in the grocery store—some grocers keep them with the vitamins and supplements whereas others shelve them with the baking supplies. Store opened packages in the refrigerator.

ADJUSTING TO NEW FOODS

Foods like tempeh and seitan probably seem weird to new vegans and, chances are, you may not even know how to pronounce them (*tem*-pay and *say*-tan). Your taste buds will likely need some time to adjust, so keep trying if you don't love these ingredients at first.

A good way to get yourself used to new foods is to try different methods of cooking them. If you didn't like that sautéed broccoli, roast it in the oven next time. You can also pair a new food with an already-loved sauce or condiment. If you liked barbecued pork as an omnivore, try barbecued seitan as a vegan.

THE FUNDAMENTALS

Before you dive into the recipes, it's helpful to know how to cook foundational ingredients, such as beans and grains. You can use canned beans and store-bought precooked grains if you like, but making them yourself is more economical and much tastier. I recommend batch cooking ingredients at the beginning of the week and storing them in the freezer until you're ready to cook. All cooked beans and grains freeze well. Just wait for them to cool, measure the portions you'll need for your recipes, and store them in airtight containers or sealed freezer bags.

It's best to store dried beans and grains in airtight containers in a cool, dry place, such as your pantry (grains can even go in the freezer). It's also a good idea to label them with the date purchased. They'll keep for many months, but, after a year or so, they'll lose nutrients and won't be as easy to cook or digest.

HOW TO COOK LENTILS

Lentils are a favorite of mine because they have all the health benefits of beans with a lot less work. They're high in protein, iron, fiber, and folic acid and they have a hearty, meaty texture. They're incredibly versatile, too. Add them to soups, throw them into salads, use them as a taco filling, or mash and mold them into burgers.

Lentils don't require any presoaking, but you should rinse them before cooking, checking for small stones and debris. Lentils cook really quickly, so they're a great option for busy weeknights.

TYPE OF LENTIL (1 CUP DRIED)	WATER	COOKING TIME	YIELD
Brown	2¼ cups	15 to 20 minutes	2¼ cups
Green	2 cups	20 to 25 minutes	2 cups
Red	3 cups	10 to 20 minutes	2½ cups
Yellow	3 cups	15 to 20 minutes	2½ cups

HOW TO COOK BEANS

Beans are an important part of a vegan diet. Not only are they loaded with protein, they also contain iron, B vitamins, and lots of fiber.

To prepare your dried beans, place them in a colander and check for pebbles and debris, then give them a good rinse. Place your beans in a bowl with enough water to cover them and soak for 4 to 8 hours. The larger the bean, the longer the soaking time should be. You know that old rhyme about beans being a magical fruit? Well, soaking your beans will make them more digestible and help reduce the cooking time. Discard the water after soaking them and rinse the beans again.

When it's time to cook, place your soaked beans in a pot with 3 to 4 cups of water. Bring the pot to a boil over medium-high heat and skim off any foam that may form on the surface of the water. Lower the heat to medium-low and simmer the beans uncovered. The cooking times in the chart on page 13 are approximate. If you live at a high altitude, it may take longer for your beans to cook. They'll be done when they're tender, so the best guide is to taste them.

If you want to add salt to your beans, don't do so until the last few minutes of cooking. Adding salt too early in the cooking process will cause the beans to toughen, and they won't soak up water as easily. You can also add bay leaves and garlic cloves to the water at the beginning of cooking for extra flavor.

TYPE OF BEAN (1 CUP DRIED)	WATER	COOKING TIME	YIELD
Black	4 cups	1 to 1¼ hours	2¼ cups
Black-Eyed Peas	3 cups	1 hour	2 cups
Cannellini	3 cups	45 minutes	2½ cups
Chickpeas (Garbanzo Beans)	4 cups	1 to 2 hours	2 cups
Fava	3 cups	40 to 50 minutes	1⅔ cups
Great Northern	3½ cups	1½ hours	2⅔ cups
Kidney	3 cups	1 hour	2¼ cups
Lima	4 cups	45 minutes to 1 hour	2 cups
Navy	3 cups	45 minutes to 1 hour	2⅔ cups
Pinto	3 cups	1 to 1½ hours	2¾ cups

HOW TO COOK GRAINS

You might think of grains as just a side dish or a vehicle to serve stir-fries with, but they're pretty versatile. Eat them for breakfast as a porridge, add them to soups, make them into salads, or use them as a stuffing.

As with beans and lentils, it's good to place your grains in a colander and check them for small stones or debris, then rinse them with cold water. You can soak some grains in water before cooking to soften them and help with digestibility, but it's not necessary. I suggest soaking only heartier grains that take longer to cook, such as brown rice and barley, as opposed to the quicker-cooking grains, such as couscous and oats.

To cook grains, add them, along with the amount of water needed, to a pot over medium-high heat and bring to a boil. Immediately reduce the heat to medium-low, cover the pot, and simmer until all the water has been absorbed and the grains are tender. Once the grains are cooked, turn off the heat and let them rest for 5 to 10 minutes. Fluff with a fork before serving.

To infuse more flavor into your grains, add a little salt to the cooking water in the beginning. You can also add bay leaves, garlic cloves, and spices to the water. I like to throw a veggie bouillon cube or two into the cooking water when cooking rice or quinoa.

TYPE OF GRAIN (1 CUP DRIED)	WATER	COOKING TIME	YIELD
Barley (Hulled)	3 cups	50 to 60 minutes	3½ cups
Barley (Pearled)	2 cups	25 to 30 minutes	4 cups
Brown Rice	2½ cups	35 to 45 minutes	3 cups
Couscous	1 cup	5 to 10 minutes	4 cups
Oats (Rolled)	2 cups	5 to 10 minutes	2 cups
Oats (Steel Cut)	3 cups	20 to 30 minutes	3 cups
Quinoa	2 cups	12 to 15 minutes	3 cups
White Rice	2 cups	15 to 20 minutes	3 cups
Wild Rice	3 cups	45 to 50 minutes	3½ cups

HOW TO PRESS TOFU

Firm and extra-firm tofu come packed in water, which you'll need to press out before cooking. Warning: If you skip this step, your tofu will fall apart when it's cooked and its water will dilute the flavors of your recipe. Yikes!

You can buy a fancy tofu press, but you really don't need one. The best way to press tofu is to wrap it in a clean kitchen towel, put it on a plate, and place something heavy on top of it, such as a cast iron skillet or a plate with a few cans of beans stacked on top. Leave it for about 20 minutes so the water can seep out. You can also put it in a colander and leave it in the refrigerator for a few hours. As water will be draining out, place the colander over something that can collect the water, like a bowl or plate.

HOW TO SOAK NUTS

As I mentioned, raw nuts are the key to lush, creamy sauces and savory, cheesy flavors. But to achieve that silky texture when blended, the nuts need to be soaked ahead of time to soften them. Make sure you use raw, unroasted, unsalted nuts without skins. Skinning them yourself can take days, so when buying nuts that usually have skins (such as almonds), look for the blanched kind.

To soak nuts, simply place them in a bowl with twice as much room-temperature filtered water. So, if you're soaking 1 cup of nuts, you'll need 2 cups of water.

Some nuts, such as cashews and pine nuts, are naturally softer than others—soak these for 2 to 4 hours. Harder nuts, such as almonds, hazelnuts, and macadamias, need a longer soaking time—between 8 and 12 hours. Leave them at room temperature or place them in the refrigerator. After soaking, be sure to drain the water and rinse the nuts.

A much quicker way to soften any type of nut is to boil it. Simply place the nuts in a pot with enough water to cover them, bring to a boil, and boil over medium-high heat for 20 minutes. Then drain and rinse. You will lose some nutritional value by boiling the nuts, however—it's a tradeoff for the time you save.

WHAT ABOUT NUTRITION?

There's a joke that once you go vegan, everyone around you suddenly turns into a nutritionist, lecturing you about iron and calcium. Prepare yourself to be asked, "Where do you get your protein?" because it's going to happen *a lot*.

I assure you that the plant world is full of nutrients—including protein!—and you won't have to spend too much time fretting over vitamins and minerals. If you're eating a balanced diet with a variety of vegetables and fruits, whole grains, nuts, and beans, chances are you're in good shape.

Beans, tofu, tempeh, and nuts are loaded with protein, as well as iron and B vitamins. Grains contain iron, vitamins B and E, and dietary fiber. If you're worried about calcium, make sure you're eating plenty of leafy green vegetables, because they're chock-full of it (as well as iron, magnesium, potassium, zinc, and vitamins A, C, E, and K). Each vegetable has its own unique nutritional profile, but, in general, they contain plenty of vitamins and minerals, as well as fiber, phytonutrients, and antioxidants.

The one nutrient vegans do need to supplement is vitamin B_{12}, because it's not naturally found in plant sources. In *How Not to Die*, Michael Greger, MD, recommends that adults under 65 take 2,500 mcg of vitamin B_{12} *each week*. It can be difficult to absorb B_{12} as we get older, so he recommends that people over 65 increase their intake to 1,000 mcg *a day*. If you're concerned about your B_{12} levels—or the level of any other nutrient—ask your doctor for a blood test.

After each recipe in this book, you'll see its nutritional breakdown, including how much protein and iron it contains.

MEAL PLANNING

Meal planning simply means sitting down and figuring out what you're going to eat for the week. You can get super specific about it, writing down every meal for each day along with snacks and drinks, or you can simply plan your lunches and dinners to make your work day run a little more smoothly. Meal planning can be especially helpful when transitioning to a new way of eating.

Some people take their meal planning a step further and prep food for the whole week on Sunday. This can be as simple as batch cooking beans and grains and storing them in the freezer to be used in meals throughout the week. Or it can be cooking all your meals for the week and portioning them into containers so meals are ready to go when you are. Choose what's best for you.

WHY MEAL PLANS HELP

Adjusting to a new way of eating can be stressful, especially when juggling work and family. Planning your meals can take some of the pressure off because you won't have to think of something to cook for dinner on the fly. It makes lunchtime at work easier, too. When I worked in an office, the local restaurants had slim pickings when it came to vegan options. Bringing your own lunch makes you less likely to revert to old ways of eating because you're hungry and pressed for time.

Meal planning can save both time and money at the grocery store, too. At some point, we've all wandered aimlessly through the aisles, unsure of what to buy. We've grabbed certain veggies with high hopes of cooking them in something—though we don't know exactly what—only to let them rot in the produce drawer (I'm looking at you, cucumbers!). As you plan your meals for the week, make a grocery list and stick to it when you're at the store.

MAKING MEAL PLANNING EASY

When meal planning, it's good to start with a cookbook (oh look, you've already got one!), a calendar, and a shopping list. Bookmark the recipes you're going to make, mark them on the calendar, and add the ingredients to your shopping list— easy peasy!

I'm a big fan of cooking once and eating twice, so when making your meal plan for the week, it's helpful to plan for leftovers. Look for a main dish recipe that will reheat well (the leftover-friendly labels in this book are a good sign) so you can have it for dinner two nights in a row or eat the leftovers for lunch the next day. It's also useful to look for meals that use the same beans or grains, so you can batch cook and have your staples ready to go.

Before you head to the store, check the refrigerator to see what needs to be used up. Look through your pantry to see what dried goods and canned foods you have on hand, so you don't end up buying repeat ingredients.

STARTER MEAL PLANS

Here are two meal plan options to help you try out eating vegan at your own pace.

TIPTOE IN: ONE VEGAN MEAL PER DAY

Try this week-long plan with one vegan meal per day to ease in.

Monday: Poké Bowl (page 105) for dinner
Tuesday: Poké Bowl leftovers for lunch
Wednesday: Sweet and Sour Tofu (page 99) for dinner
Thursday: Sweet and Sour Tofu leftovers for lunch
Friday: Black Bean Tacos (page 83) for dinner
Saturday: Veggie-Loaded Tofu Scramble (page 32) for brunch
Sunday: Baked Ziti (page 110) for dinner

SNACKS (Choose one or two for each day)			
Cucumber slices and hummus	Crispy Roasted Chickpeas (page 60)	Carrot and Celery Sticks with Tofu Ranch Dressing (page 133)	Hearts of Palm Ceviche (page 62)
Grapes	Spinach Artichoke Dip (page 61)	Buffalo Cauliflower (page 66)	Peanut butter on toast
Almonds	Banana	Apple	Olives

DEEP DIVE: 3 VEGAN MEALS PER DAY

Ready to take the plunge? Try this plan for one week of strictly plant-based meals.

	Breakfast	Lunch	Dinner
M	Strawberry Avocado Green Smoothie (page 24)	Buffalo Chickpea Salad (page 40)	Poké Bowl (page 105)
T	Lemon Raspberry Overnight Chia Pudding (page 25)	Leftover Poké Bowl	Stuffed Peppers (page 103)
W	Leftover Lemon Raspberry Overnight Chia Pudding	Leftover Buffalo Chickpea Salad	Sweet and Sour Tofu (page 99)
TH	Loaded Avocado Toast (page 29)	Leftover Sweet and Sour Tofu	Leftover Stuffed Peppers
F	Vanilla Chai-Spiced Oatmeal (page 30)	Chickpea Salad Sandwich (page 73)	Black Bean Tacos (page 83)
S	Veggie-Loaded Tofu Scramble (page 32)	Red Lentil Chili (page 53)	Fully Loaded Vegetable Pizza (page 85)
SUN	French Toast (page 37)	Leftover Red Lentil Chili	Baked Ziti (page 110)

Deep Dive Shopping List (including snacks that are recipes in the book)

Produce

- Arugula (2 cups)
- Avocados (5)
- Banana (1)
- Bell pepper, green (1)
- Bell peppers, red (8)
- Cabbage, red (1 head)
- Carrots (4)
- Cauliflower (1 head)
- Celery (1 bunch)
- Cilantro (1 bunch), or parsley
- Corn kernels, fresh or frozen (1 cup)
- Cucumber (1)
- Garlic (1 head)
- Ginger (1 small branch)
- Kale, curly (1 bunch)
- Lemons (10)
- Limes (4)
- Mushrooms, cremini (8 ounces)
- Mushrooms, white button (5 ounces)
- Onion, red (2)
- Onion, sweet (4)
- Onions, yellow (3)
- Parsley (1 small bunch)
- Raspberries (½ cup)
- Romaine lettuce (3 heads)
- Spinach (2 cups)
- Scallions (1 bunch)
- Strawberries (3 cups)
- Tomatoes (4)

Grains

- Bread of choice (1 loaf)
- Bread, whole grain (8 slices)
- Pasta, ziti or penne, uncooked (1 pound)
- Quinoa, dried (1½ cups)
- Rice, white or brown, raw (4 cups)
- Rolled oats, uncooked (2 cups)
- Tortillas, corn (6)

Beans

- Black beans (1 [15-ounce] can)
- Chickpeas (3 [15-ounce] cans)
- Edamame, fresh or frozen, shelled (1 cup)
- Lentils, brown (1 [15-ounce] can)
- Lentils, dried red (1½ cups)

Nuts and Seeds

- Almonds, blanched (2 cups)
- Cashews, raw (2¾ cups)
- Chia seeds (½ cup)
- Macadamia nuts, unsalted (2 cups)
- Peanut butter (1 [16-ounce] jar)
- Sesame seeds (any size container)

Oils and Acids

- Oil: olive, sesame, vegetable
- Tamari, low-sodium, or soy sauce
- Vinegar: apple cider, rice

Herbs and Spices

- Black pepper
- Basil, dried
- Cardamom, ground
- Chili powder
- Cinnamon, ground
- Cloves, ground
- Cumin, ground
- Dill, dried
- Garlic powder
- Ginger, ground
- Mustard, dried
- Onion powder
- Red pepper flakes
- Salt
- Turmeric, ground

Canned and Jarred Goods

- Artichoke hearts (1 [14-ounce] can)
- Dill pickles (1 [24-ounce] jar), or relish
- Hearts of palm (2 [14-ounce] cans)
- Marinara sauce (2 [24-ounce] jars)
- Pineapple, diced (1 [20-ounce] can)
- Tomatoes, diced (2 [14-ounce] cans)
- Tomato sauce (1 cup)

Condiments

- Hot sauce
- Mustard, Dijon
- Sriracha
- Tamari, low-sodium, or soy sauce

Refrigerated and Frozen

- Miso, white
- Nut milk (80 ounces)
- Spinach, frozen (1 [10-ounce] bag)
- Tofu, extra-firm (2 [14-ounce] containers)
- Tofu, firm (1 [14-ounce] container)
- Tofu, silken (2 [12-ounce] packages)

Other

- Cornstarch
- Flour, all-purpose
- Maple syrup
- Nutritional yeast
- Sugar, granulated
- Tapioca starch
- Vanilla extract
- Vegetable stock (1 [32-ounce] carton)
- Yeast, active dry (1 [0.25-ounce] package)

CHAPTER 3

BREAKFAST

Because breakfast is often centered on things like eggs, bacon, sausage, and dairy milk, many people aren't sure what to eat for their morning meal once they've gone vegan. I assure you there are plenty of satisfying plant-based foods to start your day. In this chapter, you'll get recipes for quick and easy weekday breakfasts that will help fuel you through busy mornings, as well as a few recipes perfect for leisurely week-end brunches.

STRAWBERRY AVOCADO GREEN SMOOTHIE

SERVES 2 / PREP TIME: 5 MINUTES
GLUTEN-FREE • PLAN AHEAD

Is there anything more *vegan* than a green smoothie? It's a deliciously easy way to start the day, and it provides a boost of nutrients to get you through your morning. Frozen bananas add a touch of sweet creaminess to this recipe. As soon as you get home from the grocery store, peel and slice your bananas and pop them in the freezer so you have them ready to go in the morning.

3 cups frozen strawberries
2 cups Nut Milk of choice (page 130), or store-bought nondairy milk
2 cups tightly packed fresh spinach
1 frozen banana, peeled and sliced
1 avocado, peeled, halved, and pitted
1 teaspoon maple syrup, or agave nectar (optional)

In a blender, combine the strawberries, nut milk, spinach, banana, avocado, and maple syrup (if using). Blend on high speed until smooth and creamy.

Variation tip: Green smoothies can have endless flavor variations. Instead of strawberries, use any type of berry, or peaches, mangoes, pineapples, or a combination of your favorite fruits. Add ½ teaspoon ground cinnamon or ground ginger or 1 teaspoon vanilla extract for a little extra something.

Per serving: Calories: 357; Fat: 20g; Carbohydrates: 41g; Fiber: 15g; Protein: 7g; Sodium: 393mg; Iron: 4mg

LEMON RASPBERRY OVERNIGHT CHIA PUDDING

SERVES 2 / PREP TIME: 10 MINUTES, PLUS CHILLING TIME

GLUTEN-FREE • PLAN AHEAD

When you hear the word *chia*, you might think of those terracotta "pets" with their fuzzy green coats. But did you know that not only is that green fuzz edible, the seeds are, too? In fact, chia seeds are loaded with nutrients, including fiber, protein, calcium, magnesium, and omega-3 fatty acids. They turn gel-like when soaked in water, which makes a perfect base for this pudding.

2 cups Nut Milk of choice (page 130), or store-bought nondairy milk
½ cup chia seeds
½ cup freshly squeezed lemon juice
2 tablespoons maple syrup, or agave nectar
½ cup fresh raspberries

1. In a medium bowl, stir together the nut milk, chia seeds, lemon juice, and maple syrup. Use a fork to make sure the seeds are well mixed into the milk.

2. Cover the bowl and refrigerate for 4 hours, or overnight, to set.

3. In the morning, serve the pudding topped with the raspberries.

Variation tip: You can customize chia pudding to your liking. If you'd prefer chocolate pudding, omit the lemon juice and mix in ¼ cup unsweetened cocoa powder. If vanilla is more your thing, mix in 1 teaspoon vanilla extract. Top with any type of fresh fruit that suits your fancy. Chopped nuts, toasted coconut, seeds, and cacao nibs are also great toppings.

Per serving: *Calories: 442; Fat: 24g; Carbohydrates: 45g; Fiber: 24g; Protein: 13g; Sodium: 383mg; Iron: 7mg*

BREAKFAST TACOS

MAKES 8 TACOS / PREP TIME: 10 MINUTES / COOK TIME: 10 MINUTES
LEFTOVER-FRIENDLY • NUT-FREE • PLAN AHEAD

How can your day go wrong when you start it with tacos? They're fast and filling—and much more fun to eat that than a bowl of cold cereal. It hasn't been scientifically proven, but I'm willing to bet that those who have tacos for breakfast are happier throughout the day than those who don't. Load these up with your favorite fixings. I like to add sliced jalapeños, salsa, shredded romaine lettuce, and hot sauce.

1 (14-ounce) container extra-firm tofu, drained and pressed (see page 15)
2 tablespoons nutritional yeast
1 teaspoon chili powder
½ teaspoon garlic powder
½ teaspoon ground cumin
½ teaspoon salt
¼ teaspoon red pepper flakes
1 teaspoon vegetable oil
1 (15-ounce) can black beans, drained and rinsed, or 1½ cups cooked black beans (see page 13)
8 taco shells, or 6-inch corn tortillas, warmed
½ cup Tofu Sour Cream (page 132), or store-bought nondairy sour cream
1 ripe avocado, peeled, halved, pitted, and cut into slices

1. In a large bowl, crumble the tofu into bite-size pieces using your hands or a large fork. Add the nutritional yeast, chili powder, garlic powder, cumin, salt, and red pepper flakes and toss to coat the tofu well.

2. In a large saute pan or skillet over medium-high heat, heat the vegetable oil. Add the tofu and cook for about 5 minutes, stirring frequently.

Continued >

3. Add the black beans and cook for 5 minutes more, or until the tofu begins to brown and the beans are heated through.

4. To assemble your tacos, fill each taco shell with a large spoonful of the tofu and bean mixture. Top with the sour cream and avocado.

First-Timer tip: Make the filling in advance and reheat it in the morning. Either give it a minute or two in the microwave or cook it in a skillet over medium-high heat for 3 to 4 minutes.

Per serving: *Calories: 218; Fat: 10g; Carbohydrates: 24g; Fiber: 7g; Protein: 11g; Sodium: 186mg; Iron: 2mg*

LOADED AVOCADO TOAST

SERVES 2 / PREP TIME: 15 MINUTES
PLAN AHEAD

A few years ago, a millionaire real estate mogul had a little advice for those struggling to save money to buy a house: Stop buying avocado toast. Although I doubt the money saved from buying avocado toast would actually put a dent on a down payment, I do agree with the part about buying it. The type that restaurants serve can sometimes be nothing but mashed avocado on dry bread, so I like to make my own at home and jazz it up with extra toppings.

1 large avocado, peeled, halved, pitted, and diced
1 teaspoon freshly squeezed lemon juice
⅛ teaspoon salt
2 slices whole-grain bread, or gluten-free vegan bread, toasted
2 tablespoons Cashew Cream Cheese (page 138), or store-bought nondairy
    cream cheese
1 tomato, thinly sliced
¼ teaspoon red pepper flakes (optional)

1. In a medium bowl, combine the avocado, lemon juice, and salt. Using a fork, mash the avocado while mixing in the other ingredients.

2. Spread your toasted bread slices with the cream cheese, followed by the mashed avocado and tomato slices. Sprinkle on the red pepper flakes (if using).

Variation tip: Instead of cream cheese and tomato, give your avocado toast a Mediterranean flair with Tofu Feta (page 137) and thinly sliced cucumber. Or try black beans, hot sauce, and a little lime juice. This toast is also great with nondairy pesto and Almond Parmesan Crumbles (page 136).

Per serving: *Calories: 310; Fat: 22g; Carbohydrates: 23g; Fiber: 10g; Protein: 8g; Sodium: 403mg; Iron: 2mg*

VANILLA CHAI-SPICED OATMEAL

SERVES 4 / PREP TIME: 5 MINUTES / COOK TIME: 15 MINUTES
GLUTEN-FREE • PLAN AHEAD

In India, the word *chai* means tea, but we Westerners know it as a spiced tea made with cinnamon, ginger, cloves, cardamom, and black pepper, usually served as a latte. It's warming and comforting, especially in the chilly autumn and winter months. If you want to put the tea back in your chai, use 2 cups brewed black tea rather than water when making this oatmeal.

2 cups water
2 cups Nut Milk of choice (page 130), or store-bought nondairy milk
2 cups rolled oats
2 tablespoons maple syrup
1 teaspoon vanilla extract
1 teaspoon ground cinnamon
½ teaspoon ground ginger
½ teaspoon ground cloves
½ teaspoon ground cardamom
Pinch freshly ground black pepper

1. In a medium saucepan over medium-high heat, combine the water, nut milk, and oats. Bring to a boil, then turn the heat to medium.

2. Stir in the maple syrup, vanilla, cinnamon, ginger, cloves, cardamom, and pepper. Cook for 5 to 10 minutes, stirring occasionally, or until the oatmeal has reached your desired consistency.

First-Timer tip: If you want to save time in the morning, make overnight oats. Omit the water from this recipe and place all the other ingredients in a large jar or a container with a lid. Give it a good shake to mix everything together and pop it in the refrigerator overnight. Breakfast will be ready and waiting for you in the morning.

Per serving: *Calories: 244; Fat: 6g; Carbohydrates: 39g; Fiber: 6g; Protein: 7g; Sodium: 184mg; Iron: 3mg*

APPLE CINNAMON GRANOLA

MAKES ABOUT 2 CUPS / PREP TIME: 10 MINUTES / COOK TIME: 25 MINUTES
GLUTEN-FREE • LEFTOVER-FRIENDLY

I grew up thinking of granola as a health food, but once I got older, I realized that it's loaded with oil and processed sugar. That's why I make my own using nut butter and maple syrup. Add it to parfaits alongside nondairy yogurt and fresh fruit, pair it with Nut Milk (page 130) as a breakfast cereal, or snack on it by itself.

¼ cup almond butter
¼ cup maple syrup
¼ cup unsweetened applesauce
2 teaspoons ground cinnamon
1 teaspoon vanilla extract
1½ cups rolled oats
½ cup sunflower seeds
½ cup chopped pecans
1 cup chopped dried apples

1. Preheat the oven to 325°F. Line a large baking sheet with parchment paper.

2. In a medium bowl, whisk the almond butter, maple, syrup, applesauce, cinnamon, and vanilla.

3. In a large bowl, stir together the oats, sunflower seeds, and pecans. Pour the almond butter mixture into the bowl and stir to combine everything. Spread the mixture on the prepared baking sheet in an even layer.

4. Bake for 20 to 25 minutes, stirring at the 10-minute mark. The granola is done when the oats are golden brown. Check the granola frequently to make sure it doesn't burn.

5. Remove from the oven and stir in the dried apples. The granola may be soft, but it will crisp as it cools. Let cool completely before serving.

6. Store in an airtight container at room temperature for up to 1 month.

Variation tip: Use any combination of nuts and dried fruit you like. Try almonds and dried blueberries or walnuts and dried cranberries.

Per serving (¼ cup): *Calories: 267; Fat: 15g; Carbohydrates: 31g; Fiber: 5g; Protein: 6g; Sodium: 48mg; Iron: 2mg*

VEGGIE-LOADED TOFU SCRAMBLE

SERVES 4 / PREP TIME: 15 MINUTES / COOK TIME: 20 MINUTES
GLUTEN-FREE • LEFTOVER-FRIENDLY • NUT-FREE

I like to make this tofu scramble on the weekends, my cats waiting patiently behind me, hoping I'll drop a little nooch on the floor for them to snack on. It's easy to customize your scramble with your favorite vegetables. Try it with spinach and tomatoes or zucchini and Swiss chard. Serve it with home fries and toast for the ultimate weekend brunch.

1 (14-ounce) container extra-firm tofu, drained and pressed (see page 15)
2 tablespoons nutritional yeast
1 teaspoon ground turmeric
½ teaspoon onion powder
½ teaspoon salt
½ teaspoon freshly ground black pepper
1 teaspoon vegetable oil
½ cup diced yellow onion (about ½ small onion)
5 ounces mushrooms, sliced (about 2 cups)
1 red bell pepper, seeded and chopped
2 cups chopped curly kale (3 or 4 leaves), stemmed

1. In a large bowl, crumble the tofu into bite-size pieces using your hands or a large fork. Add the nutritional yeast, turmeric, onion powder, salt, and pepper. Toss to coat the tofu well.

2. In a large saute pan or skillet over medium-high heat, heat the vegetable oil. Add the onion and cook for about 5 minutes, stirring frequently, until it begins to brown.

3. Add the mushrooms, red bell pepper, and kale. Cook for 5 minutes, or until the veggies begin to soften.

4. Add the tofu to the skillet and cook for 8 to 10 minutes, stirring frequently, or until the tofu begins to brown.

First-Timer tip: Tofu scramble reheats well, so it's a good meal to prep on Sundays for breakfasts throughout the week.

Per serving: *Calories: 152; Fat: 6g; Carbohydrates: 14g; Fiber: 5g; Protein: 15g; Sodium: 323mg; Iron: 4mg*

BANANA BREAD PANCAKES

SERVES 4 / PREP TIME: 10 MINUTES / COOK TIME: 15 MINUTES
PLAN AHEAD

This may sound crazy, but once pancakes have been stacked on a plate and topped with loads of syrup, they get a little mushy for my taste. So I like to add fruit and nuts to give them a little texture. The combination of bananas and walnuts in this recipe really does the trick for me.

1½ cups all-purpose flour
1 tablespoon baking powder
1 teaspoon ground cinnamon
¼ teaspoon salt
1 large ripe banana, peeled and mashed
1½ cups Nut Milk of choice (page 130), or store-bought nondairy milk
2 tablespoons maple syrup
2 teaspoons vegetable oil, plus more for cooking
1 teaspoon vanilla extract
½ cup chopped walnuts

1. In a large bowl, whisk the flour, baking powder, cinnamon, and salt to combine.

2. In a medium bowl, whisk the banana, nut milk, maple syrup, vegetable oil, and vanilla. Pour the wet ingredients into the dry ingredients and stir until they are just combined. Don't overmix the batter. Gently fold in the walnuts.

3. Lightly coat a large griddle or skillet with vegetable oil and place it over medium-high heat.

4. When the griddle is hot, spoon about ½ cup of batter onto it. Cook until small bubbles appear on the top and the edges look dry, 2 to 3 minutes. Flip the pancake and cook for 1 to 2 minutes more. Remove the pancake to a plate and repeat with the remaining batter. Cover the cooked pancakes so they stay hot while the rest are cooking.

Variation tip: To make carrot cake pancakes, skip the banana and use 1 carrot, grated, instead. Add ¼ cup raisins to the mixture when folding in the walnuts.

Per serving: *Calories: 418; Fat: 17g; Carbohydrates: 59g; Fiber: 4g; Protein: 9g; Sodium: 288mg; Iron: 4mg*

SPINACH QUICHE

SERVES 8 / PREP TIME: 15 MINUTES / COOK TIME: 45 MINUTES
LEFTOVER-FRIENDLY • PLAN AHEAD

Quiche is a brunch classic in my house, because it's so easy to customize. You can throw pretty much any sautéed vegetable into the mixture. I like to add cooked mushrooms and zucchini, or chopped jarred artichoke hearts and olives. If you're in the mood for a frittata rather than a quiche, skip the crust and bake the tofu mixture in a lightly greased 9-inch pie dish or tart pan.

1 (14-ounce) container extra-firm tofu, drained and pressed (see page 15)
3 tablespoons nutritional yeast
3 tablespoons freshly squeezed lemon juice
2 tablespoons Nut Milk of choice (page 130), or store-bought nondairy milk
1 tablespoon cornstarch
1 teaspoon ground turmeric
½ teaspoon garlic powder
½ teaspoon onion powder
½ teaspoon dried basil
½ teaspoon dried thyme
½ teaspoon red pepper flakes
½ teaspoon salt
¼ teaspoon freshly ground black pepper
1 (16-ounce) bag fresh baby spinach
1 recipe Pastry Dough (page 141), or store-bought nondairy piecrust, uncooked

1. Preheat the oven to 350°F.

2. Crumble the tofu into the bowl of a food processer. Add the nutritional yeast, lemon juice, nut milk, cornstarch, turmeric, garlic powder, onion powder, basil, thyme, red pepper flakes, salt, and pepper. Process until the mixture is thick and resembles ricotta.

3. Add the spinach and pulse until it's chopped and mixed throughout the tofu. You may need to do this in batches, depending on the size of your food processor. Pour the tofu mixture into the prepared piecrust.

Continued >

4. Bake for 40 to 45 minutes, or until the filling is firm and the crust is golden brown. Let the quiche sit for 5 minutes before slicing and serving.

First-Timer tip: If you don't have a food processor, don't worry! Crumble the tofu into a large bowl and add the nutritional yeast, lemon juice, nut milk, and cornstarch along with all the herbs and spices. Using a potato masher or large wooden spoon, mash the tofu, mixing it with the rest of the ingredients. Coarsely chop the spinach and fold it into the tofu mixture until it's well incorporated. You can even use frozen spinach instead of fresh; just defrost it at room temperature first and drain off as much of the water as possible. Finish the quiche as instructed.

Per serving: *Calories: 159; Fat: 8g; Carbohydrates: 15g; Fiber: 4g; Protein: 10g; Sodium: 304mg; Iron: 3mg*

FRENCH TOAST

SERVES 4 / PREP TIME: 10 MINUTES / COOK TIME: 10 MINUTES
PLAN AHEAD

French toast was a breakfast favorite before I went vegan. After giving up eggs, I had no idea how to make it, so I went French toast–less for a time. Then, while on vacation, I stayed in a vegan-friendly B&B and my hosts served up a big plate of it for breakfast. I was slightly suspicious as to how they could have cooked such delicious French toast without eggs—so I asked. The chef proudly explained that he used a vegan vanilla pudding mix to make it—which, I admit, is a pretty genius move. That pudding mix was primarily cornstarch, so here I've skipped the mix and used cornstarch and vanilla extract.

1 cup Nut Milk of choice (page 130), or store-bought nondairy milk
¼ cup maple syrup
2 tablespoons cornstarch
1 teaspoon vanilla extract
½ teaspoon ground cinnamon
¼ teaspoon salt
4 to 6 slices whole-grain bread, or gluten-free vegan bread
Vegetable oil, for cooking

1. In a medium bowl, whisk the nut milk, maple syrup, cornstarch, vanilla, cinnamon, and salt to combine. Pour the mixture into a shallow dish. Place the bread into the batter, letting it soak up the mixture for about 1 minute.

2. Lightly coat a large griddle or skillet with vegetable oil and place it over medium-high heat.

3. When the griddle is hot, place the soaked bread on it and cook for 3 to 4 minutes, or until the bottom is golden brown. Flip and cook the other side for 3 to 4 minutes, or until golden brown.

Variation tip: To make stuffed French toast, place a slice of cooked French toast on a plate and spread on a thick layer of Cashew Cream Cheese (page 138). Top with another slice of French toast and ¼ cup sliced strawberries.

Per serving: *Calories: 191; Fat: 6g; Carbohydrates: 29g; Fiber: 3g; Protein: 4g; Sodium: 372mg; Iron: 1mg*

CHAPTER 4

SALADS, SOUPS, AND STEWS

After discovering that I don't eat meat, someone once said, "You must be really good at making salad." Actually, I *am* really good at making salad, but it's not because I'm vegan—it's because I like salad. Vegans eat way more than salad, but it is a good option if you're trying to fit more healthy veggies into your diet. To make salads interesting, mix up your ingredients with seasonal produce, add cooked grains and beans, and experiment with different dressings. In the winter months, use those same ingredients in a warming soup or stew.

BUFFALO CHICKPEA SALAD

SERVES 2 AS A MAIN DISH, 4 AS A SIDE / PREP TIME: 15 MINUTES
GLUTEN-FREE • NUT-FREE • PLAN AHEAD

I should warn you—this salad is so good, you might find yourself craving it all day. "Do people actually crave salad?" you ask. Yes, it is possible, especially when that salad is made with spicy Buffalo sauce and cool, creamy ranch dressing. You could end up packing a salad for lunch and making a little extra so there are leftovers for dinner . . . or for when you wake up with a hankering for it for breakfast. Don't say you weren't warned!

1 (15-ounce) can chickpeas, drained and rinsed, or 1½ cups cooked chickpeas (see page 13)
3 tablespoons hot sauce
1 tablespoon vegetable oil, or vegetable stock
6 cups chopped romaine lettuce (about 1 large head)
1 cup shredded red cabbage
2 celery stalks, chopped
1 carrot, grated or shredded
1 cup Tofu Ranch Dressing (page 133), or store-bought nondairy ranch dressing

1. In a medium bowl, toss the chickpeas, hot sauce, and vegetable oil to coat.

2. In a large bowl, toss the lettuce, red cabbage, celery, and carrot to combine.

3. Add the dressing and toss to coat well.

4. Serve the salad topped with the spicy chickpeas.

Variation tip: If you'd like all the taste of a salad in a portable hand-held meal, turn this salad into a wrap. Simply place your salad on a large tortilla and roll it up, tucking in the sides as you go.

Per serving: *Calories: 489; Fat: 27g; Carbohydrates: 49g; Fiber: 13g; Protein: 13g; Sodium: 514mg; Iron: 9mg*

CAESAR WEDGE SALAD

SERVES 2 AS A MAIN DISH, 4 AS A SIDE / PREP TIME: 15 MINUTES
30 MINUTES OR LESS • PLAN AHEAD

Caesar dressing used to be my go-to choice—until the day I turned the bottle around and read the label, only to realize it was made with anchovies. Fish in salad dressing—who knew? The lessons I learned that day were two-fold: First, read the ingredients for *everything*; and second, it would be a lot less worrisome to make my own salad dressings at home. This vegan version of Caesar dressing gets its salty flavor from capers.

For the dressing
1 cup silken tofu
3 tablespoons freshly squeezed lemon juice
2 teaspoons capers
1 teaspoon Dijon mustard
1 teaspoon white miso
½ teaspoon garlic powder
½ teaspoon salt

For the salad
2 romaine lettuce hearts, stem ends
   trimmed, hearts sliced lengthwise
1 tomato, diced
1 cup croutons
⅓ cup Almond Parmesan Crumbles
   (page 136), or store-bought
   nondairy parmesan

To make the dressing
In a blender, combine the silken tofu, lemon juice, capers, Dijon, miso, garlic powder, and salt. Blend until smooth and creamy. Set aside.

To make the salad
1. Place the lettuce, cut-side up, on a plate and drizzle it with the dressing.
2. Top with the tomato, croutons, and almond parmesan crumbles.

Fun fact: Caesar salad has nothing to do with Julius Caesar. It was invented by Italian chef Caesar Cardini, who owned restaurants in both California and Mexico. Legend has it that his restaurant's kitchen was looking bare after a busy Fourth of July weekend, so he threw together what he had on hand and served it to his friends.

Substitution tip: Use the Crispy Roasted Chickpeas (page 60) instead of croutons to make this salad gluten-free.

Per serving: Calories: 273; Fat: 4g; Carbohydrates: 26g; Fiber: 2g; Protein: 27g; Sodium: 1529mg; Iron: 2mg

APPLE SPINACH SALAD

SERVES 2 AS A MAIN DISH, 4 AS A SIDE / PREP TIME: 15 MINUTES
GLUTEN-FREE • PLAN AHEAD

Lettuce gets all the glory when it comes to salads, but I think it's high time spinach received some of that leafy green praise. To give this salad a little more oomph, toss in some roasted squash, cooked rice, and crumbled tempeh bacon. This recipe has a fall feel to it, but you can bring it into spring by swapping the apple for sliced fresh strawberries, using dried blueberries instead of cranberries, and substituting chopped almonds for pecans.

For the dressing
2 tablespoons extra-virgin olive oil
2 tablespoons balsamic vinegar
1 teaspoon Dijon mustard
1 teaspoon maple syrup
¼ teaspoon salt
Pinch freshly ground black pepper

For the salad
1 (5-ounce) bag fresh baby spinach (about 8 cups)
1 apple, any variety, cored and diced
1 cup Tofu Feta (page 137), or store-bought nondairy feta
½ cup dried cranberries
½ cup chopped pecans

To make the dressing
In a small bowl, whisk the olive oil, vinegar, Dijon, maple syrup, salt, and pepper until blended. Set aside.

To make the salad
1. In a large bowl, toss the spinach, apple, and tofu feta to combine.
2. Drizzle with the dressing and toss to coat well.
3. Top with the dried cranberries and pecans.

First-Timer tip: If you're not eating your salad right away, toss the chopped apple pieces in lemon juice to prevent browning.

Per serving: *Calories: 539; Fat: 37g; Carbohydrates: 49g; Fiber: 10g; Protein: 10g; Sodium: 381mg; Iron: 7mg*

PEANUT-Y MANDARIN SALAD

SERVES 2 AS A MAIN DISH, 4 AS A SIDE / PREP TIME: 15 MINUTES
30 MINUTES OR LESS • GLUTEN-FREE

I created the first version of this salad a few years ago for a quick and easy weeknight cooking class. It comes together in a flash, especially if you use canned mandarin oranges. You can reduce prep time even more by using jarred peanut sauce, which is usually found near the soy sauce in the grocery store. If you'd like to bulk up the salad a little, toss in cubed baked tofu, which you can find next to the regular tofu in the grocery store.

For the dressing
⅓ cup full-fat coconut milk
¼ cup peanut butter
2 garlic cloves, minced
1 teaspoon maple syrup
½-inch piece fresh ginger, peeled and coarsely chopped
¼ teaspoon red pepper flakes

For the salad
5 ounces spring mix salad greens (about 8 cups)
3 fresh mandarin oranges, peeled and segmented, or 2 (11-ounce) cans, drained
½ cup shelled edamame, fresh or frozen and thawed
¼ cup chopped peanuts
2 scallions, sliced

To make the dressing
In a blender, combine the coconut milk, peanut butter, garlic, maple syrup, ginger, and red pepper flakes. Blend until smooth and creamy. Set aside.

To make the salad
1. In a large bowl, toss the salad greens, oranges, and edamame to combine.
2. Drizzle on the dressing and toss to coat well.
3. Top with the peanuts and scallions.

Substitution tip: If you have a peanut allergy, substitute almond or cashew butter. Or, if you can't eat nuts at all, try sunflower butter.

Per serving: *Calories: 480; Fat: 35g; Carbohydrates: 33g; Fiber: 8g; Protein: 18g; Sodium: 167mg; Iron: 8mg*

BROCCOLI SLAW WITH GINGER MISO DRESSING

SERVES 2 AS A MAIN DISH, 4 AS A SIDE / PREP TIME: 15 MINUTES

30 MINUTES OR LESS

For this dressing, I was inspired by the famous carrot ginger dressing from Dojo, the New York City cheap eats spot beloved in the 1990s. I could drink that stuff with a straw! It's the reason this salad is way better than traditional coleslaw. You can serve it as a side for veggie burgers and tofu dogs, but it also makes a great meal on its own with some chickpeas or cubed baked tofu.

For the dressing
2 tablespoons white miso
2 tablespoons tahini
2 tablespoons rice vinegar, or apple cider vinegar
2 tablespoons water
1 tablespoon maple syrup
1 tablespoon low-sodium tamari, or soy sauce
1-inch piece fresh ginger, peeled and coarsely chopped

For the salad
1 large head broccoli (about 1½ pounds), florets chopped into bite-size pieces, stalk peeled and grated
2 carrots, grated
2 scallions, sliced
¼ cup chopped or slivered almonds

To make the dressing
In a blender, combine the miso, tahini, vinegar, water, maple syrup, tamari, and ginger. Blend until smooth and creamy. Set aside.

To make the salad
1. In a large bowl, toss the broccoli, carrots, and scallions to combine.
2. Add the dressing to the bowl and toss to coat well.
3. Top with the almonds.

Substitution tip: To reduce prep time, use packaged broccoli slaw. You can also use grated or shredded cabbage instead of broccoli.

Per serving: Calories: 379; Fat: 16g; Carbohydrates: 48g; Fiber: 14g; Protein: 18g; Sodium: 1116mg; Iron: 5mg

QUINOA TABBOULEH

SERVES 2 AS A MAIN DISH, 4 AS A SIDE / PREP TIME: 15 MINUTES
GLUTEN-FREE • LEFTOVER-FRIENDLY • NUT-FREE • PLAN AHEAD

I love Middle Eastern restaurants because they always have accidentally vegan dishes, such as falafel, baba ghanoush, and tabbouleh. Tabbouleh is traditionally made with bulgur wheat, but I use quinoa because it cooks up quicker, and because it's a great option for those on a gluten-free diet. If you don't mind straying from the traditional, add some chickpeas, Tofu Feta (page 137), and sliced Kalamata olives to this salad. Serve it with pita bread and hummus for the full Middle Eastern experience.

For the dressing
¼ cup freshly squeezed lemon juice
¼ cup extra-virgin olive oil
1 garlic clove, minced
½ teaspoon salt
½ teaspoon freshly ground black pepper

For the salad
3 cups cooked quinoa (see page 14)
1½ cups chopped fresh flat-
  leaf parsley
½ cup chopped fresh mint
3 scallions, sliced
1 tomato, finely diced

To make the dressing
In a small bowl, whisk the lemon juice, olive oil, garlic, salt, and pepper until combined. Set aside.

To make the salad
1. In a large bowl, toss the quinoa, parsley, mint, scallions, and tomato until well combined.
2. Add the dressing to the salad and toss to coat well.

Substitution tip: Use 3 cups cooked bulgur or couscous instead of quinoa. You can also use cauliflower rice as a sneaky way to get more veggies into your meal.

Per serving: *Calories: 605; Fat: 31g; Carbohydrates: 69g; Fiber: 12g; Protein: 16g; Sodium: 650mg; Iron: 6mg*

CORN CHOWDER

SERVES 4 / PREP TIME: 15 MINUTES / COOK TIME: 30 MINUTES
LEFTOVER-FRIENDLY · PLAN AHEAD

There are a few types of clam chowder: New England style is made with a creamy broth, whereas Manhattan has a tomato base. Corn chowder is made with . . . well, corn, of course, in a cream base. It's a great late-summer soup, when fresh corn is readily available. You can make this soup any time of year, though, thanks to the convenience of frozen corn.

2 teaspoons vegetable oil
1 small yellow onion, chopped
2 garlic cloves, minced
2 celery stalks, chopped
2 carrots, chopped
2 tablespoons flour of choice
2 cups vegetable stock
2 cups Nut Milk of choice (page 130), or store-bought nondairy milk
2 cups corn, fresh or frozen and thawed
1 pound Yukon gold potatoes, cut into 1-inch cubes
1 teaspoon dried thyme
Salt
Freshly ground black pepper

1. In a large stockpot over medium heat, heat the vegetable oil. Add the onion, garlic, celery, and carrots. Cook for about 10 minutes, or until the vegetables begin to soften. Sprinkle the vegetables with the flour and stir to coat.

2. Increase the heat to medium-high and stir in the vegetable stock, nut milk, corn, potatoes, and thyme. Bring the mixture to a boil, reduce the heat once again to medium, and simmer the soup for 10 to 15 minutes, or until the potatoes are tender and the soup has thickened slightly. Taste and season with salt and pepper.

First-Timer tip: If you prefer your chowder on the creamier side, blend half the soup in a blender until smooth and creamy and stir it back into the pot before seasoning with salt and pepper. If you have an immersion blender, give it a few pulses in the pot until the soup reaches the consistency you like.

Per serving: *Calories: 221; Fat: 6g; Carbohydrates: 38g; Fiber: 7g; Protein: 5g; Sodium: 457mg; Iron: 2mg*

CHICKPEA NOODLE SOUP

SERVES 6 / PREP TIME: 15 MINUTES / COOK TIME: 30 MINUTES
LEFTOVER-FRIENDLY • NUT-FREE

I grew up on super salty canned chicken noodle soup, as many children of the 1970s did. On Saturday afternoons and sick days, I would slurp down bowls of it while wearing pajamas and watching cartoons. This grown-up vegan version cuts down on the salt using low-sodium vegetable stock and swaps the chicken for chickpeas, but it's just as slurpable as that soup from my childhood. Though the pasta choice is up to you, this soup works best with bite-size varieties such as elbow macaroni or rotini. Pajamas and cartoons are optional.

1 tablespoon vegetable oil
1 small yellow onion, chopped
4 carrots, chopped
4 celery stalks, chopped
2 garlic cloves, minced
8 cups low-sodium vegetable stock
6 ounces dried pasta, shape of choice (about 3 cups elbows or rotini)
1 (15-ounce) can chickpeas, drained and rinsed, or 1½ cups cooked chickpeas (see page 13)
½ teaspoon dried basil
½ teaspoon dried oregano
½ teaspoon dried thyme
½ teaspoon dried sage
Salt
Freshly ground black pepper

1. In a large stockpot over medium-high heat, heat the vegetable oil. Add the onion and cook for about 5 minutes, stirring occasionally, until it begins to soften. Add the carrots, celery, and garlic. Cook for about 5 minutes more, or until the vegetables begin to soften.

2. Add the vegetable stock, pasta, chickpeas, basil, oregano, thyme, and sage to the pot. Bring the mixture to a boil, then lower the heat to maintain a simmer. Cook for 10 to 12 minutes until the pasta is tender, stirring frequently.

3. Remove from the heat. Taste and season with salt and pepper.

Substitution tip: If you have poultry seasoning on hand, use 2 teaspoons of it instead of the dried herbs. Poultry seasoning doesn't actually contain any chicken—it's a blend of herbs and spices typically used to season poultry and is safe for vegans.

Per serving: *Calories: 240; Fat: 4g; Carbohydrates: 44g; Fiber: 7g; Protein: 9g; Sodium: 227mg; Iron: 4mg*

BLACK BEAN SOUP

SERVES 4 / PREP TIME: 10 MINUTES / COOK TIME: 25 MINUTES
GLUTEN-FREE • LEFTOVER-FRIENDLY • NUT-FREE

I've learned to be careful when ordering black bean soup in restaurants because it can sometimes be made with ham or bacon. (Why do people put bacon in everything?) If you find yourself missing that smoky flavor, add a little smoked paprika to this soup, or toss in some crumbled tempeh bacon. Serve with diced avocado and a dollop of Tofu Sour Cream (page 132). The soup is great as is, or you can pair it with cooked rice for a hearty main course. It freezes well, too, so it's a great dish for weekend meal prep.

2 teaspoons vegetable oil
1 small yellow onion, chopped
3 garlic cloves, minced
2 (15-ounce) cans black beans, drained and rinsed
1 (15-ounce) can diced tomatoes, undrained
2 cups vegetable stock
2 teaspoons chili powder
1 teaspoon ground cumin
½ teaspoon red pepper flakes
Salt
Freshly ground black pepper

1. In a large stockpot over medium-high heat, heat the vegetable oil. Add the onion and cook for about 5 minutes, stirring occasionally, until the onion begins to soften. Add the garlic and cook for 1 to 2 minutes more.

2. Add the black beans, tomatoes and their juices, vegetable stock, chili powder, cumin, and red pepper flakes to the pot. Bring the mixture to a boil, then reduce the heat to medium and simmer for 15 minutes.

3. Transfer 1 cup of soup to a blender and blend until smooth. Pour the blended soup back into the pot and stir to combine. Taste and season with salt and pepper.

First-Timer tip: If you have an immersion blender, use it in step 3. Remove the pot from the heat and give the immersion blender a few pulses in the soup until it reaches your desired texture.

Per serving: *Calories: 231; Fat: 4g; Carbohydrates: 39g; Fiber: 14g; Protein: 13g; Sodium: 300mg; Iron: 4mg*

CURRIED SQUASH SOUP

SERVES 6 / PREP TIME: 10 MINUTES / COOK TIME: 30 MINUTES
GLUTEN-FREE • LEFTOVER-FRIENDLY • NUT-FREE

Creamy bisque-style soups are my favorite. In this one, coconut milk adds a bit of lusciousness and curry powder gives it complexity. If you're feeling ambitious, add cooked cannellini beans and fresh spinach after blending for a more stew-like dish. Try swirling a little Tofu Sour Cream (page 132) into your soup just before serving for a little extra yum.

1 tablespoon vegetable oil
1 small onion, chopped
2 garlic cloves, minced
2 pounds butternut squash, peeled, seeded, and cut into 1-inch pieces
4 cups vegetable stock
1 (14-ounce) can coconut milk
1 tablespoon curry powder
1 teaspoon ground ginger
½ teaspoon red pepper flakes (optional)
Salt
Freshly ground black pepper

1. In a large stockpot over medium-high heat, heat the vegetable oil. Add the onion and cook for about 5 minutes, stirring occasionally, until it begins to soften. Add the garlic and cook for 1 to 2 minutes more.

2. Stir in the butternut squash, vegetable stock, coconut milk, curry powder, ginger, and red pepper flakes (if using). Bring the soup to a boil, then reduce the heat to medium and simmer for 12 to 15 minutes, or until the squash softens.

3. Remove the soup from the heat and let cool slightly. Transfer the soup to a blender and purée until smooth and creamy. Depending on the size of your blender, you may need to do this in batches. If you have an immersion blender, use it right in the pot to blend your soup.

4. Return the soup to the pot and cook over medium-high heat for 2 to 3 minutes until heated through. Taste and season with salt and pepper.

Per serving: *Calories: 353; Fat: 25g; Carbohydrates: 35g; Fiber: 6g; Protein: 5g; Sodium: 543mg; Iron: 5mg*

RED LENTIL CHILI

SERVES 4 / PREP TIME: 10 MINUTES / COOK TIME: 35 MINUTES
GLUTEN-FREE • LEFTOVER-FRIENDLY • NUT-FREE

Who doesn't love chili? It's hearty and filling, and a great dish for hiding veggies from picky eaters. If you have extra time, add some diced carrot, cubed butternut squash, and even a handful of finely chopped kale. Sure, you can serve this dish in a bowl, but pouring it over a baked sweet potato kicks dinner up a notch. Serve your chili topped with diced avocado, jalapeño slices, Tofu Sour Cream (page 132), and Almond Parmesan Crumbles (page 136) for some extra flavor pop.

2 teaspoons vegetable oil
1 small yellow onion, chopped
1 red bell pepper, seeded and chopped
3 garlic cloves, minced
3 cups vegetable stock
1 cup dried red lentils
1 (14-ounce) can diced tomatoes, undrained
2 tablespoons chili powder
Salt
Freshly ground black pepper

1. In a large stockpot over medium-high heat, heat the vegetable oil. Add the onion and red bell pepper. Cook for about 5 minutes, stirring occasionally, until the vegetables begin to soften. Add the garlic and cook for 1 to 2 minutes more.

2. Stir in the vegetable stock, lentils, tomatoes, and chili powder. Bring the chili to a boil, then reduce the heat to medium-low, cover the pot, and simmer for about 20 minutes, or until the lentils are fully cooked and the chili has thickened.

3. Taste and season with salt and pepper.

First-Timer tip: If you have a slow cooker, combine the ingredients in it, cover the cooker, and cook the chili on low heat for 8 hours.

Per serving: *Calories: 246; Fat: 4g; Carbohydrates: 41g; Fiber: 18g; Protein: 14g; Sodium: 446mg; Iron: 5mg*

MISO RAMEN

SERVES 4 / PREP TIME: 15 MINUTES / COOK TIME: 20 MINUTES
LEFTOVER-FRIENDLY • NUT-FREE

Because they're so inexpensive, instant ramen noodles are often the food of choice for those just starting out in the world of adulting. In my college days, I bought a package to try and I was *not* a fan. They might be cheap, but you get what you pay for. I went years thinking I didn't like ramen, but then I tried a grown-up version and I was hooked. Plain ramen noodles may be difficult to find, so you can buy the cheap flavored kind in a pinch and just discard the seasoning packets.

¼ cup white miso
8 cups vegetable stock, divided
2 teaspoons vegetable oil
3 scallions, sliced
4 garlic cloves, minced
2-inch piece fresh ginger, peeled and minced
3 (3-ounce) packages plain ramen noodles
4 ounces shiitake mushrooms, sliced (about 1½ cups)
2 cups chopped baby bok choy
1 cup snap peas
1 tablespoon low-sodium tamari, or soy sauce
Salt
Freshly ground black pepper

1. In a large bowl, whisk the miso and 4 cups of vegetable stock to blend. Set aside.

2. In a large stockpot over medium heat, heat the vegetable oil. Add the scallions, garlic, and ginger. Cook for 2 to 3 minutes, just until everything begins to soften.

3. Turn the heat to medium-high. Add the remaining 4 cups of vegetable stock to the pot along with the noodles, mushrooms, bok choy, snap peas, and tamari.

4. Bring the mixture to a boil, then lower the heat to medium and simmer for about 10 minutes, or until the noodles have softened and the snap peas are crisp-tender. Stir in the miso mixture. Taste and season with salt and pepper.

First-Timer tip: Miso is fermented, which means it contains live, active probiotic cultures, like the ones in yogurt. Boiling miso kills those cultures, so it's best to add miso to warm stock to retain its health benefits. Shiitake mushrooms can be a little pricy, but you can save money by buying the dried variety. You'll need just 1 or 2 ounces dried mushrooms. To reconstitute them, place them in a medium bowl and add enough boiling water to cover them. Let soak for about 15 minutes. Once they've expanded and softened, rinse them with clean water. You can save the soaking water and use it as stock in the soup.

Per serving: *Calories: 395; Fat: 14g; Carbohydrates: 55g; Fiber: 6g; Protein: 13g; Sodium: 3709mg; Iron: 4mg*

SEITAN BOURGUIGNON

SERVES 4 / PREP TIME: 15 MINUTES / COOK TIME: 35 MINUTES
LEFTOVER-FRIENDLY • NUT-FREE • PLAN AHEAD

Bourguignon is a French stew traditionally made with beef braised in red wine. This vegan version uses meaty seitan, but you can use store-bought vegan beef, if you prefer. If you're not in a hurry to have dinner, let it simmer longer to ramp up the flavor. Some people like to serve their bourguignon over pasta or mashed potatoes; I prefer it in a big bowl with a piece of crusty French bread.

2 teaspoons vegetable oil
1 small yellow onion, chopped
8 ounces Seitan (page 144), or store-bought seitan, chopped into bite-size pieces (about 2 cups)
8 ounces cremini mushrooms, or white button mushrooms, chopped (about 3 cups)
1 carrot, chopped
3 garlic cloves, minced
2 tablespoons flour of choice
2 cups dry red wine
1 cup vegetable stock
2 tablespoons tomato paste
1 teaspoon dried thyme
½ teaspoon dried rosemary
Salt
Freshly ground black pepper

1. In a large stockpot over medium-high heat, heat the vegetable oil. Add the onion and cook for about 5 minutes, stirring occasionally, until it begins to soften. Add the seitan, mushrooms, carrot, and garlic to the pot. Cook, stirring frequently, until the vegetables have softened, about 10 more minutes.

2. Sprinkle the mixture with the flour and stir to coat.

3. Stir in the red wine, vegetable stock, tomato paste, thyme, and rosemary. Bring the mixture to a boil, then reduce the heat to medium-low and simmer for 10 to 15 minutes, or until the stew has thickened slightly and the alcohol has cooked off.

4. Taste and season with salt and pepper.

First-Timer tip: You'd think a beverage made from fermented grapes would be vegan, but actually, not all wines are. Some winemakers use ingredients such as isinglass (fish bladders), albumen (from eggs), casein (from milk), and gelatin (trust me—you don't want to know where gelatin comes from) to filter their vino. To find out if your wine is vegan, contact the manufacturer or check Barnivore.com.

Per serving: *Calories: 383; Fat: 5g; Carbohydrates: 11g; Fiber: 4g; Protein: 45g; Sodium: 1088mg; Iron: 3mg*

CHAPTER 5

SNACKS AND SIDES

In this chapter, you'll find quick eats for at-home or on-the-go snacking, appetizers that are perfect for parties, and side dishes that pair well with the main dishes in chapter 7. If you know you tend to feel hungry between meals, it's a good idea to keep some snacks ready to go so you don't fall into the trap of hitting up the office snack machine, where there might not be too many vegan choices (and the chances of healthy options are super slim).

CRISPY ROASTED CHICKPEAS

SERVES 4 / PREP TIME: 5 MINUTES / COOK TIME: 35 MINUTES

GLUTEN-FREE • LEFTOVER-FRIENDLY • NUT-FREE

I'm not really sure how I first realized that roasting chickpeas turns them into a crunchy snack, but once I started making them, I became addicted. This was years ago, and I felt like they were my little secret. Then, somehow, my snack secret was blown, and packages of roasted chickpeas started appearing everywhere. They're much tastier when you cook them yourself, though, so I keep making them at home. You can munch on them as a snack, toss them into salads instead of croutons, or use them to garnish soups.

1 (15-ounce) can chickpeas, drained and rinsed, or 1½ cups cooked chickpeas (see page 13)
1 teaspoon vegetable oil
1 teaspoon freshly squeezed lemon juice
1 teaspoon garlic powder
1 teaspoon onion powder
½ teaspoon salt

1. Preheat the oven to 425°F. Line a large baking sheet with parchment paper.

2. In a medium bowl, combine the chickpeas, vegetable oil, and lemon juice. Toss to coat.

3. Add the garlic powder, onion powder, and salt and toss again to coat the chickpeas well. Spread the chickpeas on the prepared baking sheet in an even layer.

4. Bake for 15 minutes. Roll the chickpeas around on the baking sheet, then bake for 15 to 20 minutes more, or until they're crisp. Keep an eye on them so they don't burn.

Variation tip: You can easily change the flavor of your chickpeas by mixing up the seasonings. For spicy chickpeas, use 1 teaspoon vegetable oil, 1 teaspoon freshly squeezed lime juice, 1 teaspoon chili powder, 1 teaspoon cumin, ½ teaspoon cayenne pepper, and ½ teaspoon salt. For ranch chickpeas, use 1 teaspoon vegetable oil, 1 teaspoon apple cider vinegar, ½ teaspoon dried dill, ½ teaspoon dried thyme, ½ teaspoon onion powder, and ½ teaspoon garlic powder.

Per serving: Calories: 116; Fat: 3g; Carbohydrates: 18g; Fiber: 5g; Protein: 6g; Sodium: 296mg; Iron: 2mg

SPINACH ARTICHOKE DIP

MAKES ABOUT 4 CUPS / PREP TIME: 10 MINUTES / COOK TIME: 20 MINUTES
GLUTEN-FREE • LEFTOVER-FRIENDLY • PLAN AHEAD

With two veggies in the name, you'd think that spinach artichoke dip would be a healthy snack, but it's usually swimming with fatty dairy products. The vegan version is made with healthier, dairy-free sour cream and cream cheese. Don't skimp on the nooch, as it gives the dip its cheesy taste. This snack is always a hit, but honestly, you might not want to share it. Bake up a batch and have a party for one! Serve it with chips, cut fresh veggies, or chunks of fresh bread.

Vegetable oil, for preparing the baking dish
1 cup Cashew Cream Cheese (page 138), or store-bought nondairy cream cheese
½ cup Tofu Sour Cream (page 132), or store-bought nondairy sour cream
½ cup nutritional yeast
½ teaspoon garlic powder
½ teaspoon onion powder
1 (14-ounce) can artichoke hearts, drained and chopped
1 (10-ounce) bag frozen spinach, thawed, drained, and chopped
Salt
Freshly ground black pepper

1. Preheat the oven to 375°F. Lightly coat a small (8-by-11-inch) baking dish with vegetable oil.

2. In a medium bowl, stir together the cashew cream cheese, tofu sour cream, nutritional yeast, garlic powder, and onion powder. Gently fold in the artichokes and spinach. Spread the mixture in the prepared baking dish.

3. Bake for 20 minutes, or until bubbly and brown.

First-Timer tip: You can thaw frozen spinach on the counter at room temperature or by microwaving it in a bowl for 1 to 2 minutes. It's important to get as much of the water out as possible or your dip will be watery. To do this, place the thawed spinach in a colander in the sink and use your hands to squeeze out the water. You can also wrap it in paper towels and squeeze it over a colander. The colander will catch any spinach if the paper towels tear.

Per serving (½ cup): *Calories: 213; Fat: 13g; Carbohydrates: 16g; Fiber: 8g; Protein: 12g; Sodium: 234mg; Iron: 3mg*

HEARTS OF PALM CEVICHE

SERVES 4 / PREP TIME: 15 MINUTES

30 MINUTES OR LESS • GLUTEN-FREE • LEFTOVER-FRIENDLY • NUT-FREE

Ceviche is a raw seafood dish made of chopped fish, peppers, onions, and citrus juice—sort of a fishy salsa. This vegan version is made with sliced hearts of palm and is easy to customize to suit whatever ingredients you have on hand. Feel free to add diced jalapeño or chopped olives. I've had it as an appetizer in restaurants alongside tortilla chips, but you can also serve it on a bed of lettuce as a salad or in tortillas as tacos.

1 (14-ounce) can hearts of palm, drained and cut into slices
1 ripe avocado, peeled, halved, pitted, and chopped
1 tomato, diced
¼ cup diced red onion
2 tablespoons chopped fresh cilantro, or parsley
¼ cup freshly squeezed lime juice
2 tablespoons extra-virgin olive oil
Salt
Freshly ground black pepper

1. In a large bowl, stir together the hearts of palm, avocado, tomato, red onion, and cilantro.

2. In a small bowl, whisk the lime juice and olive oil to blend. Pour the dressing over the vegetables and gently mix to coat the vegetables well. Taste and season with salt and pepper.

3. You can eat this ceviche right away, or marinate it in the refrigerator for an hour or so. Keep refrigerated in an airtight container for up to 2 days.

Fun fact: Hearts of palm are harvested from certain types of palm trees. They have a delicate flavor and are a great addition to salads. Because of their flaky texture, they're often used to mimic seafood in vegan cuisine. You can usually find them in cans or jars in the canned vegetable section of the grocery store. Check the label to make sure they're sustainably harvested. Sometimes whole trees are cut down to harvest hearts of palm, but it's also possible to harvest them from multi-stemmed plants.

Per serving: Calories: 175; Fat: 14g; Carbohydrates: 12g; Fiber: 6g; Protein: 4g; Sodium: 468mg; Iron: 4mg

STRAWBERRY AND FETA BRUSCHETTA

SERVES 4 / PREP TIME: 20 MINUTES / COOK TIME: 10 MINUTES
NUT-FREE • PLAN AHEAD

I know the combination of strawberries, balsamic vinegar, basil, and black pepper sounds weird—but trust me when I tell you it's amazing. The vinegar and pepper intensify the sweet flavor of the strawberry and the basil provides a savory complement. Tofu Feta (page 137) adds a nice salty punch to the mix. Instead of spooning the mixture onto bread, you can go gluten-free and serve it as a salad. Thank me later.

1 (16-inch) baguette, cut into ½-inch slices
1 tablespoon olive oil
1 pound fresh strawberries, stemmed and sliced
1 cup Tofu Feta (page 137), or store-bought nondairy feta
2 tablespoons sliced fresh basil
2 tablespoons balsamic vinegar
½ teaspoon freshly ground black pepper

1. Preheat the oven to 350°F. Line a large baking sheet with parchment paper.
2. Place the baguette slices on the prepared baking sheet and lightly brush or drizzle them with olive oil.
3. Bake for 5 to 10 minutes, or until the slices are lightly browned.
4. In a medium bowl, stir together the strawberries, tofu feta, basil, vinegar, and pepper. Spoon the strawberry mixture onto the toasted bread slices and serve immediately.

Substitution tip: Instead of strawberries, use chopped fresh peaches, nectarines, or plums. If you can find fruit-flavored balsamic, use it here. It'll add a nice depth of flavor.

Per serving: Calories: 277; Fat: 8g; Carbohydrates: 42g; Fiber: 4g; Protein: 13g; Sodium: 377mg; Iron: 4mg

MISO-GLAZED MAPLE SWEET POTATO FRIES

SERVES 4 / PREP TIME: 10 MINUTES / COOK TIME: 30 MINUTES
GLUTEN-FREE • LEFTOVER-FRIENDLY • NUT-FREE

If you've ever ordered sweet potato fries in a restaurant, you already know they're thin, crispy, carby perfection. But if you've tried to make them at home, chances are they were a limp disappointment. The secret to getting them crisp is cornstarch, which reduces moisture. Waiting until after they've cooked to add salt helps, too. If you're not in a hurry, you can crisp your fries even more by soaking the cut sweet potato wedges in cold water for about 1 hour beforehand, then pat them dry before sprinkling with cornstarch.

2 sweet potatoes (about 2 pounds), cut into thin (1-inch) wedges
2 tablespoons cornstarch
¼ cup maple syrup
2 tablespoons white miso
2 tablespoons apple cider vinegar
Salt
Freshly ground black pepper

1. Preheat the oven to 425°F. Line a large baking sheet with parchment paper.

2. In large bowl, combine the sweet potatoes and cornstarch. Toss to coat well.

3. In a small bowl, whisk the maple syrup, miso, and vinegar to blend. Pour the mixture over the sweet potatoes and toss them to coat well. Spread the sweet potatoes on the prepared baking sheet in a single layer.

4. Bake for 25 to 30 minutes, flipping the fries at the halfway point, or until lightly browned. Season with salt and pepper.

Fun fact: What we usually refer to as "yams" here in the Unites States are actually sweet potatoes. Real yams have tough, bumpy, brown skin that looks a little like tree bark, and their flesh is white and not so sweet. They're common in Caribbean and West African cuisine.

Per serving: *Calories: 280; Fat: 1g; Carbohydrates: 65g; Fiber: 7g; Protein: 5g; Sodium: 486mg; Iron: 2mg*

BUFFALO CAULIFLOWER

SERVES 4 / PREP TIME: 15 MINUTES / COOK TIME: 35 MINUTES

PLAN AHEAD

Cauliflower has become the "it" vegetable in recent years, taking the place of rice, mashed potatoes, and even meat in recipes like this one. You can serve these finger lickin' good nuggets as a snack or an appetizer, add them to salads, or turn them into tacos.

1 cup flour of choice
1 cup Nut Milk of choice (page 130), or store-bought nondairy milk
2 teaspoons garlic powder
½ teaspoon salt
Freshly ground black pepper
1 head cauliflower, chopped into bite-size florets (about 4 cups)
½ cup hot sauce
2 tablespoons olive oil
1 cup Tofu Ranch Dressing (page 133), or store-bought nondairy ranch dressing

1. Preheat the oven to 450°F. Line a large baking sheet with parchment paper. Set aside.

2. In a large bowl, stir together the flour, nut milk, garlic powder, and salt. Season with pepper. Add the cauliflower florets and toss until well coated. Tap each piece gently on the side of the bowl to remove any excess batter. Place the pieces on the prepared baking sheet.

3. Bake for 20 to 25 minutes, flipping each piece at the halfway point, or until the cauliflower begins to brown and slightly crisps around the edges.

4. While the cauliflower bakes, in a small bowl, whisk the hot sauce and olive oil to blend. Drizzle the sauce over the cauliflower pieces and return them to the oven for 5 to 10 minutes more.

5. Serve the cauliflower hot with the dressing for dipping.

Fun fact: Buffalo sauce has nothing to do with flying wild oxen. It originated in Buffalo, New York—though the story as to exactly where in that city is disputed.

Per serving: Calories: 323; Fat: 15g; Carbohydrates: 41g; Fiber: 7g; Protein: 9g; Sodium: 1290mg; Iron: 3mg

PEANUT-Y SEITAN SKEWERS

SERVES 4 / PREP TIME: 10 MINUTES, PLUS MARINATING TIME / COOK TIME: 15 MINUTES
PLAN AHEAD

Based on a Thai food favorite, these skewers are a fun appetizer or party snack, although honestly, I could make a meal out of them. You'll need 8 to 10 skewers, about 8 inches long. If you're using wooden or bamboo skewers, soak them in water for about 30 minutes before using so they don't burn in the oven. You can use store-bought vegan beef instead of seitan in this recipe, or chopped portobello mushrooms if you're gluten-free.

For the seitan skewers
1 pound Seitan (page 144), or store-bought seitan, chopped into bite-size pieces (about 4 cups)
½ cup vegetable stock
¼ cup low-sodium tamari, or soy sauce
2 garlic cloves, minced, or ½ teaspoon garlic powder
1-inch piece fresh ginger, peeled and coarsely chopped, or 1 teaspoon ground ginger

For the peanut sauce
½ cup peanut butter
½ cup Nut Milk of choice (page 130), or store-bought nondairy milk
1 tablespoon low-sodium tamari, or soy sauce
1 tablespoon freshly squeezed lime juice
¼ teaspoon red pepper flakes

To make the seitan skewers
1. Thread the seitan pieces on skewers and place them in a shallow dish or large plate.

2. In a medium bowl, whisk the vegetable stock, tamari, garlic, and ginger to combine. Pour the mixture over the skewers. Let marinate for 30 to 60 minutes.

3. Preheat the oven to 375°F. Line a large baking sheet with parchment paper.

4. Remove the seitan skewers from the marinade and place them on the prepared baking sheet.

5. Bake for 15 minutes, or until they're browned and the edges begin to turn crispy.

Continued >

To make the peanut sauce

1. While the seitan bakes, in a medium bowl, whisk the peanut butter, nut milk, tamari, lime juice, and red pepper flakes until blended and smooth.

2. Drizzle the cooked skewers with the peanut sauce, or serve it on the side for dipping.

Variation tip: You can also cook these skewers on the barbecue or in a grill pan until they've browned and begin to crisp, 3 to 5 minutes per side.

Per serving: *Calories: 342; Fat: 18g; Carbohydrates: 11g; Fiber: 4g; Protein: 34g; Sodium: 1551mg; Iron: 4mg*

ROSEMARY GARLIC POTATO WEDGES

SERVES 4 / PREP TIME: 10 MINUTES / COOK TIME: 45 MINUTES
GLUTEN-FREE • LEFTOVER-FRIENDLY • NUT-FREE

What's not to love about these potato wedges? They're crispy on the outside and tender on the inside, and there's really nothing they don't pair well with. In addition to being a great companion for burgers and sandwiches, they're also delicious for breakfast instead of home fries or hash browns. They can also replace chips—try them with Spinach Artichoke Dip (page 61). Make them extra addictive by adding a generous sprinkle of Almond Parmesan Crumbles (page 136).

4 russet potatoes (about 2 pounds), each cut into 6 wedges
2 tablespoons vegetable oil
2 tablespoons freshly squeezed lemon juice
4 garlic cloves, minced
2 tablespoons minced fresh rosemary leaves
½ teaspoon salt
½ teaspoon freshly ground black pepper

1. Preheat the oven to 400°F. Line a large baking sheet with parchment paper.

2. In a large bowl, combine the potato wedges, vegetable oil, lemon juice, garlic, rosemary, salt, and pepper. Toss to coat the potatoes well. Spread the potatoes on the prepared baking sheet in a single layer.

3. Bake for 40 to 45 minutes, flipping the wedges at the halfway point, or until lightly browned and crisp around the edges.

Substitution tip: Use sweet potatoes instead of russet potatoes, if you like.

Per serving: *Calories: 251; Fat: 7g; Carbohydrates: 43g; Fiber: 4g; Protein: 5g; Sodium: 305mg; Iron: 3mg*

CHAPTER 6

HANDHELDS

Eating with your hands may be considered rude in certain circles, but not when it comes to the recipes in this chapter. In fact, I highly encourage it! Eating a taco with a knife and fork would be sacrosanct, so toss aside those utensils and have a few napkins ready. Here you'll find veganized versions of American classics, such as burgers and barbecue sandwiches, as well as international favorites like calzones, taquitos, and shawarma. These dishes are great for lunches on the go and casual dinners at home.

TOFU SALAD SANDWICHES

SERVES 6 / PREP TIME: 15 MINUTES
LEFTOVER-FRIENDLY • PLAN AHEAD

I was vegetarian for nine years before I went vegan, and egg salad sandwiches were a mainstay of my diet, because I really wasn't sure how to make sandwiches without meat. This tofu salad is reminiscent of that old favorite. Turmeric gives the tofu a yellow hue, too. Season this recipe to your liking—try a little fresh dill, or spice it up with some cayenne pepper.

1 (14-ounce) package extra-firm tofu, drained and pressed (see page 15)
2 celery stalks, finely chopped
1 scallion, finely chopped
⅓ cup Cashew Mayonnaise (page 131), or store-bought nondairy mayonnaise
1 teaspoon yellow mustard
1 teaspoon freshly squeezed lemon juice
1 teaspoon ground turmeric
Salt
Freshly ground black pepper
12 slices bread of choice
1 large tomato, sliced
6 large romaine lettuce leaves

1. Crumble the tofu into a medium bowl. Using a fork, gently mash it into small pieces.

2. Stir in the celery and scallion. Gently fold in the mayonnaise, mustard, lemon juice, and turmeric. Taste and season with salt and pepper.

3. Spoon the tofu mixture onto 6 slices of bread. Add the tomato slices and lettuce leaves and top with the remaining bread slices.

First-Timer tip: You can mix up your tofu salad by freezing the tofu beforehand, which makes it firmer and chewier. It also makes it a little spongy, which helps absorb dressings and sauces better. Just pop the package of tofu into the freezer. Once it's fully frozen, defrost it totally, then drain and press out the water as you normally would.

Per serving: *Calories: 247; Fat: 9g; Carbohydrates: 30g; Fiber: 5g; Protein: 13g; Sodium: 382mg; Iron: 13mg*

CHICKPEA SALAD SANDWICHES

SERVES 4 / PREP TIME: 15 MINUTES
LEFTOVER-FRIENDLY • PLAN AHEAD

Chickpea salad is a vegan classic—in fact, it's probably the first recipe a lot of new vegans learn to make. It's easy to hide various vegetables from veggie-phobes in this recipe, so feel free to add what you like. I sometimes include diced red peppers, chopped cucumber, sliced scallions, and even finely chopped kale. In addition to making sandwiches with this salad, you can serve a scoop or two on a bed of greens as a salad, or with crackers as a snack.

1 (15-ounce) can chickpeas, drained and rinsed, or 1½ cups cooked chickpeas (see page 13)
2 celery stalks, chopped
1 small carrot, grated or shredded
¼ cup finely chopped red onion
¼ cup finely chopped dill pickle, or pickle relish
¼ cup Cashew Mayonnaise (page 131), or store-bought nondairy mayonnaise
1 teaspoon dried dill
½ teaspoon garlic powder
½ teaspoon onion powder
Salt
Freshly ground black pepper
8 slices bread of choice
1 large tomato, sliced
4 large romaine lettuce leaves

1. Place the chickpeas in a large bowl and, using a potato masher or large fork, lightly mash them.

2. Gently stir in the celery, carrot, red onion, and dill pickle to combine everything.

3. Gently fold in the mayonnaise, dill, garlic powder, and onion powder. Taste and season with salt and pepper.

Continued >

4. Spoon the chickpea mixture onto 4 slices of bread. Add the tomato slices and lettuce leaves and top with the remaining bread slices.

Variation tip: This recipe is reminiscent of chicken salad, but you can easily turn it into a vegan "tuna" salad by omitting the dill, garlic powder, and onion powder, and using 2 teaspoons seaweed flakes instead. You can usually find seaweed flakes in the Asian food aisle of the grocery store.

Per serving: *Calories: 320; Fat: 9g; Carbohydrates: 49g; Fiber: 10g; Protein: 14g; Sodium: 510mg; Iron: 4mg*

SEITAN SHAWARMA

SERVES 4 / PREP TIME: 20 MINUTES / COOK TIME: 15 MINUTES
NUT-FREE • PLAN AHEAD

If you've ever been to a Middle Eastern restaurant, you have probably seen those very non-vegan revolving shanks of spiced meat. That meat is shawarma, and it's usually served in a wrap with sliced tomatoes, cucumbers, and tahini sauce. I will admit I've never had meat shawarma, but I've had plenty of vegan versions, and I really like them. I think you will, too!

¼ cup tahini
¼ cup water
2 tablespoons freshly squeezed lemon juice
1 teaspoon garlic powder
2 teaspoons vegetable oil
1 small red onion, thinly sliced
1 pound Seitan (page 144), or store-bought seitan, thinly sliced
½ teaspoon ground cumin
½ teaspoon ground turmeric
½ teaspoon paprika
¼ teaspoon salt
¼ teaspoon freshly ground black pepper
4 pitas, or flatbreads of choice
1 large tomato, sliced
1 cup sliced cucumber
2 cups sliced romaine lettuce

1. In a small bowl, whisk the tahini, water, lemon juice, and garlic powder to blend. Set aside.

2. In a large pan over medium-high heat, heat the vegetable oil. Add the red onion and cook for about 5 minutes, stirring frequently, until it begins to soften and brown.

3. Add the seitan, cumin, turmeric, paprika, salt, and pepper. Cook, stirring frequently, for about 10 minutes until the seitan browns and some of the edges get crispy.

Continued >

4. To assemble the sandwiches, stuff each pita with some of the seitan mixture. Add tomato and cucumber slices and romaine lettuce. Drizzle each with the tahini dressing.

Substitution tip: Swap store-bought vegan beef for the seitan, if you prefer. You can also use sliced portobello mushrooms to keep your shawarma veggie-centric.

Per serving: *Calories: 354; Fat: 12g; Carbohydrates: 41g; Fiber: 5g; Protein: 20g; Sodium: 718mg; Iron: 4mg*

CHIPOTLE SEITAN TAQUITOS

MAKES 12 TAQUITOS / PREP TIME: 15 MINUTES / COOK TIME: 15 MINUTES
LEFTOVER-FRIENDLY • PLAN AHEAD

Taquitos (sometimes called flautas) are small, rolled-up tacos—or, as I like to refer to them, little tubes of deliciousness. They're usually made with some kind of meat and deep-fried. Fried foods may taste yummy, but they're not so great for the arteries, so I like to bake my taquitos. You can serve them as is, or drizzle with Tofu Sour Cream (page 132), guacamole, and salsa. Munch on them as a snack or serve them as part of a meal.

½ cup Cashew Cream Cheese (page 138), or store-bought nondairy cream cheese
2 canned chipotle peppers in adobo sauce, minced, sauce reserved
12 (6-inch) corn tortillas
1 pound Seitan (page 144), or store-bought seitan, cut into slices

1. Preheat the oven to 400°F. Have a large baking dish or sheet nearby.

2. In a small bowl, stir together the cashew cream cheese, chipotle peppers, and 2 tablespoons of the reserved adobo sauce.

3. Place a tortilla on a clean surface and spread a line (about 2 teaspoons) of the chipotle cream cheese mixture down the middle. Top with a few slices of seitan. Roll up the tortilla as tightly as possible and place it, seam-side down, in the baking dish. Repeat with the remaining tortillas.

4. Bake for 15 minutes, or until the tortillas are crisp.

Fun fact: Chipotles are not their own type of pepper. They're actually dried, smoked jalapeños. When buying them for this recipe, look for chipotles in adobo sauce, which come in small cans found in the Mexican food section of the grocery store. You'll need both the peppers and the sauce.

Per serving (2 taquitos): *Calories: 193; Fat: 7g; Carbohydrates: 25g; Fiber: 6g; Protein: 8g; Sodium: 273mg; Iron: 1mg*

MEDITERRANEAN CHICKPEA WRAPS

SERVES 4 / PREP TIME: 15 MINUTES
NUT-FREE • PLAN AHEAD

Many years ago, Wendy's had pita sandwiches on their menu, two of which were meat-free. I was vegetarian at the time and I would frequently pick one up for lunch. My favorite was their Greek pita, stuffed with fresh veggies and feta. I must have been the only one buying it, as it was quickly discontinued. But shortly after, when I went vegan, I found myself still craving that sandwich. This wrap is my homemade vegan take on it.

¼ cup extra-virgin olive oil

2 tablespoons freshly squeezed lemon juice

1 teaspoon dried dill

1 teaspoon dried oregano

¼ teaspoon salt

1 (15-ounce) can chickpeas, drained and rinsed, or 1½ cups cooked chickpeas (see page 13)

½ cup Tofu Feta (page 137), or store-bought nondairy feta

1 cup chopped cucumber

1 large tomato, diced

¼ cup diced red onion

2 cups fresh baby spinach

4 (12-inch) tortillas, or flatbreads of choice

1. In a small bowl, whisk the olive oil, lemon juice, dill, oregano, and salt to combine.

2. In a large bowl, gently toss together the chickpeas, feta, cucumber, tomato, and red onion. Add the dressing and toss to combine.

Continued >

3. Assemble the wraps by placing ½ cup of spinach on each tortilla and topping it with ¼ of the chickpea mixture. Roll up the wrap, tucking in the sides as you go.

Substitution tip: If you'd like to keep your wraps gluten-free and you can't find gluten-free flatbread, use collard greens. You'll need 4 large collard leaves. Cut off the stem from each and shave off the thick part of the stem that's left in the center with a sharp knife. Assemble the wrap the way you would a tortilla, by filling it with the spinach and chickpea mixture and rolling the leaf, tucking in the sides as you go.

Per serving: Calories: 623; Fat: 25g; Carbohydrates: 80g; Fiber: 11g; Protein: 20g; Sodium: 814mg; Iron: 7mg

BARBECUE CHICKPEA BURGERS WITH SLAW

SERVES 4 / PREP TIME: 15 MINUTES / COOK TIME: 25 MINUTES
LEFTOVER-FRIENDLY • PLAN AHEAD

I used to think making my own veggie burgers was a daunting task. But after making them in a cooking class, I realized how easy they really are. You just need a can of beans, a binder, and some spices. Mix, shape, bake, and boom—your burger is done! They freeze well, which is super convenient. After they've baked and cooled, place a piece of parchment paper between each burger and pop them in the freezer in an airtight container. To reheat, thaw them on the counter and bake in the oven for a few minutes or pan-fry them until hot.

1 cup rolled oats
1 (15-ounce) can chickpeas, drained and rinsed, or 1½ cup cooked chickpeas (see page 13)
½ cup Barbecue Sauce (page 135), or store-bought vegan barbecue sauce, divided
1 garlic clove, minced
½ teaspoon salt
½ teaspoon freshly ground black pepper
2 cups shredded cabbage
2 carrots, grated or shredded
¼ cup Cashew Mayonnaise (page 131), or store-bought nondairy mayonnaise
4 burger buns of choice

1. Preheat the oven to 400°F. Line a large baking sheet with parchment paper.

2. In a food processor, pulse the rolled oats until they resemble a coarse meal. Add the chickpeas, ¼ cup of barbecue sauce, the garlic, salt, and pepper. Pulse until the chickpeas are mashed and everything is well combined. It's okay if there are a few whole chickpeas. Form the mixture into 4 patties and place them on the prepared baking sheet.

3. Bake the burgers for 20 to 25 minutes, flipping them at the halfway point. They should be golden brown and firm.

4. While the burgers bake, make the slaw. In a large bowl, stir together the cabbage, carrots, and mayonnaise.

Continued >

5. Serve each burger on a bun topped with 1 tablespoon of the remaining barbecue sauce and ¼ cup of slaw.

First-Timer tip: If you don't have a food processor, mash your chickpeas really well using a potato masher or large fork. Rolled oats won't mash well by hand, so use oat flour or all-purpose flour instead. Combine the mashed chickpeas, flour, barbecue sauce, garlic, salt, and pepper in a large bowl before shaping into patties.

Per serving: *Calories: 433; Fat: 10g; Carbohydrates: 73g; Fiber: 10g; Protein: 13g; Sodium: 665mg; Iron: 4mg*

BLACK BEAN TACOS

MAKES 6 TACOS / PREP TIME: 15 MINUTES / COOK TIME: 20 MINUTES
GLUTEN-FREE • NUT-FREE • PLAN AHEAD

There's a myth that tacos can only be made with meat or fish. I've had people ask me what I make tacos with because I'm vegan, but I think the question should be what I *don't* make them with. You can use beans, roasted veggies, crumbled tempeh, sliced seitan—the list goes on. You name it, I've probably stuffed it into a tortilla at some point. These tacos are super easy to make and customize, so you can celebrate Taco Tuesday any day of the week.

1 teaspoon vegetable oil
½ cup chopped yellow onion (about ½ small onion)
1 garlic clove, minced
1 (15-ounce) can black beans, drained and rinsed, or 1½ cup cooked black beans (see page 13)
¼ cup vegetable stock, or water
1½ teaspoons chili powder
½ teaspoon ground cumin
¼ teaspoon salt
6-inch corn tortillas, warmed
½ cup Tofu Sour Cream (page 132), or store-bought nondairy sour cream
1 avocado, peeled, halved, pitted, and chopped
1 tomato, diced
2 cups chopped romaine lettuce

1. In a large pan over medium-high heat, heat the vegetable oil. Add the onion and cook for about 5 minutes, stirring frequently, until it begins to soften and brown. Add the garlic and cook for 1 to 2 minutes more.

2. Stir in the black beans, vegetable stock, chili powder, cumin, and salt to combine. Reduce the heat to medium, cover the pan, and simmer for 5 to 10 minutes until all the liquid is absorbed.

Continued >

3. To assemble the tacos, fill each tortilla with some of the black bean mixture and top with a dollop of sour cream, followed by the avocado, tomato, and lettuce.

First-Timer tip: If you can't decide between hard shells or soft tortilla tacos, you don't have to! There's a taco place near me that serves their tacos with both, and I sometimes do the same at home. Simply place a soft tortilla inside a hard shell before filling with the bean mixture. The soft tortilla acts as a buffer between the filling and the hard shell, to help keep it crispy.

Per serving: *Calories: 219; Fat: 10g; Carbohydrates: 28g; Fiber: 8g; Protein: 7g; Sodium: 151mg; Iron: 2mg*

FULLY LOADED VEGETABLE PIZZA

SERVES 4 / PREP TIME: 15 MINUTES / COOK TIME: 35 MINUTES
LEFTOVER-FRIENDLY • PLAN AHEAD

Someone once told me that she could never go vegan because she couldn't give up pizza. I told her I eat pizza all the time! Before going vegan, pizza to me meant tomato sauce, cheese, and pepperoni. Now I'm much more creative, topping my pizza with different types of sauces, plenty of fresh veggies, and lots of melty Macadamia Mozzarella (page 139).

2 teaspoons vegetable oil
½ cup chopped yellow onion (about ½ small onion)
2 garlic cloves, minced
8 ounces cremini mushrooms, or white button mushrooms, sliced (about 3 cups)
1 red bell pepper, seeded and chopped
2 cups arugula, chopped
1 cup canned or jarred tomato sauce
1 recipe Pizza Dough (page 143) rolled out in a pizza pan, or 1 store-bought 16-inch pizza crust
1 cup sliced Macadamia Mozzarella (page 139), or store-bought shredded nondairy mozzarella
½ cup Almond Parmesan Crumbles (page 136), or store-bought nondairy parmesan

1. Preheat the oven to 450°F.

2. In a large pan over medium-high heat, heat the vegetable oil. Add the onion and cook for about 5 minutes, stirring frequently, until it begins to soften and brown. Add the garlic, mushrooms, and red bell pepper. Cook for 10 more minutes, or until the vegetables soften. Add the arugula to the pan and cook for 1 to 2 minutes more until wilted.

3. To prepare the pizza, evenly spread the tomato sauce over the prepared crust. Evenly distribute the vegetables over the top of the pizza. Scatter the sliced mozzarella and the almond parmesan crumbles over the pizza.

4. Bake for 12 to 15 minutes, or until the crust is golden brown and the cheese has melted. Slice and serve hot.

Per serving: *Calories: 605; Fat: 14g; Carbohydrates: 91g; Fiber: 5g; Protein: 27g; Sodium: 1332mg; Iron: 7mg*

PULLED MUSHROOM BARBECUE SANDWICHES

SERVES 4 / PREP TIME: 10 MINUTES / COOK TIME: 20 MINUTES

LEFTOVER-FRIENDLY • NUT-FREE • PLAN AHEAD

Mushrooms are one of those vegetables that people either love or hate. In teaching cooking classes, I've found that self-professed mushroom haters don't mind them when they're chopped and smothered with a sauce. I think these sandwiches would get the mushroom haters' seal of approval, but you can make them with thinly sliced Seitan (page 144) instead of mushrooms, if you like.

1 tablespoon vegetable oil
1 yellow onion, chopped
2 garlic cloves, minced
1 pound cremini mushrooms, or white button mushrooms, thinly sliced
1 cup Barbecue Sauce (page 135), or store-bought vegan barbecue sauce
Salt
Freshly ground black pepper
4 buns of choice
4 large romaine lettuce leaves
1 tomato, sliced
Pickle slices, for serving

1. In a large pan over medium-high heat, heat the vegetable oil. Add the onion and cook for about 5 minutes, stirring frequently, until it begins to soften and brown, about 5 minutes. Add the garlic and mushrooms. Cook for about 10 minutes until the mushrooms brown and soften. If there's any liquid in the pan from the mushrooms, pour it out.

2. Stir in the barbecue sauce, coating the vegetables well. Cook for about 5 minutes until the sauce is heated throughout. Season with salt and pepper.

3. To serve, divide the mixture among the 4 buns. Top each with lettuce, tomato, and pickle slices and the bun tops.

Per serving: Calories: 286; Fat: 6g; Carbohydrates: 52g; Fiber: 3g; Protein: 8g; Sodium: 938mg; Iron: 5mg

EGGPLANT PARMESAN SANDWICHES

SERVES 4 / PREP TIME: 20 MINUTES, PLUS EGGPLANT SALTING TIME / COOK TIME: 30 MINUTES

PLAN AHEAD

Eggplant parm sandwiches were a favorite of mine when I was a cheese-eating vegetarian, and I was sad to give them up after I kicked dairy. But they're back, baby! Vegans can enjoy pretty much anything parm now, thanks to the miracle that is meltable vegan mozzarella cheese. If you're not feeling sandwich-y, omit the rolls and serve the baked cheesy eggplant over pasta or even on its own in stacks.

1 eggplant

1 tablespoon salt

1 cup Nut Milk of choice (page 130), or store-bought nondairy milk

½ cup flour of choice

2 teaspoons cornstarch

1¼ cups bread crumbs of choice

1 tablespoon Italian seasoning

1 tablespoon Almond Parmesan Crumbles (page 136), or store-bought nondairy
   parmesan

½ cup sliced Macadamia Mozzarella (page 139), or store-bought nondairy mozzarella

4 hero rolls, or ciabatta buns

1 cup canned or jarred tomato sauce, warmed

1 cup arugula

1. Cut the eggplant into rounds about ½ to ¾ inch thick. You'll need 12 to 16 slices. Lay the rounds on a towel and sprinkle them with the salt. Let the slices sit for 30 to 60 minutes. Rinse them and pat them dry.

2. Preheat the oven to 425°F. Line a large baking sheet with parchment paper.

3. In a medium bowl, whisk the nut milk, flour, and cornstarch to combine. In another bowl, stir together the bread crumbs, Italian seasoning, and almond parmesan crumbles.

4. Dip each eggplant slice into the nut milk mixture and then into the bread crumb mixture, coating each slice well. Place the coated slices on the prepared baking sheet.

5. Bake the eggplant for 25 minutes, flipping each piece at the halfway mark. Place the mozzarella slices on each eggplant slice and bake for 5 minutes more, or until the cheese melts.

6. To assemble the sandwiches, place a few slices of eggplant on the bottom of each roll and top with ¼ cup of warmed tomato sauce, followed by ¼ cup of arugula and the top bun.

First-Timer tip: You may be tempted to skip the salting step, but I urge you not to. Eggplant retains a lot of water, and the salt helps pull it out so the breading will stick better and they won't be too soggy when cooked.

Per serving: *Calories: 369; Fat: 8g; Carbohydrates: 64g; Fiber: 8g; Protein: 12g; Sodium: 1338mg; Iron: 4mg*

SPINACH MUSHROOM CALZONES

MAKES 8 CALZONES / PREP TIME: 15 MINUTES / COOK TIME: 45 MINUTES

LEFTOVER-FRIENDLY • NUT-FREE • PLAN AHEAD

Calzones are basically individual folded pizzas. I think they're underrated, and they often go neglected in pizza parlors, with people opting for a big pie instead. But you can't go wrong with your own little pocket of portable pizza. Play with the fillings to make these calzones your own. Spinach and mushrooms are delish, but so are broccoli and eggplant. I stuff mine with tofu ricotta or Macadamia Mozzarella (page 139). Have extra tomato sauce on hand for dipping.

1 teaspoon vegetable oil
1 pound cremini mushrooms, or white button mushrooms, chopped
2 garlic cloves, minced
1 (5-ounce) bag fresh baby spinach, chopped (about 8 cups)
1 (14-ounce) package firm tofu, pressed and drained (see page 15)
½ cup nutritional yeast
¼ cup freshly squeezed lemon juice
1 teaspoon dried basil
½ teaspoon garlic powder
½ teaspoon salt
1 recipe Pizza Dough (page 143), or 1 pound store-bought pizza dough
Flour of choice, for dusting
½ cup canned or jarred tomato sauce

1. Preheat the oven to 425°F. Line a large baking sheet with parchment paper.

2. In a large pan over medium-high heat, heat the vegetable oil. Add the mushrooms and garlic. Cook for 10 minutes, stirring frequently, or until the mushrooms soften. Add the spinach and cook for 1 to 2 minutes more until wilted.

3. Crumble the tofu into a food processor and add the nutritional yeast, lemon juice, basil, garlic powder, and salt. Process for 2 minutes until the mixture looks like ricotta.

4. Divide the pizza dough into 8 equal pieces. Lightly flour a work surface and roll each dough portion on it into a circle about ¼ inch thick.

5. Spread about 2 tablespoons of the tofu ricotta over half of each dough circle, followed by 1 tablespoon of tomato sauce. Spoon on a little of the mushroom and spinach mixture. Fold the other half of the dough over the filling and press the edges together. Gently fold the edges over twice to seal the calzone. Place the calzone on the prepared baking sheet.

6. Bake for 25 to 30 minutes, or until golden brown.

First-Timer tip: If you don't have a food processor, place the tofu, nutritional yeast, lemon juice, basil, garlic powder, and salt in a large bowl and use a potato masher or large wooden spoon to mash everything together until it resembles ricotta.

Per serving: Calories: 317; Fat: 8g; Carbohydrates: 46g; Fiber: 7g; Protein: 20g; Sodium: 549mg; Iron: 6mg

CHAPTER 7

THE MAIN EVENT

For most American families, dinner is often a slab of meat with a veg or two on the side, so when people go vegan, they're not sure what to make for their evening meal. I hear you. When I first gave up meat, my mom heated up a bag of frozen carrots, corn, and peas and called it supper. Taking meat out of the equation encourages you to try many different foods you might not otherwise eat, like curries, pastas, casseroles, and stir-fries. I assure you they're all hearty and filling, and they'll satisfy vegans and omnivores alike.

BARBECUE TEMPEH WITH SMOKY COLLARD GREENS

SERVES 4 / PREP TIME: 10 MINUTES / COOK TIME: 20 MINUTES

LEFTOVER-FRIENDLY • NUT-FREE • PLAN AHEAD

Vegans don't eat ribs, but we do eat tempeh. It pairs really well with barbecue sauce, which caramelizes deliciously once baked. Because collards can be tough, they're often boiled for what seems like forever, but I find overcooked greens to be a little bland. If you prefer your collards softer, cook them for a few more minutes. Turn any leftovers into lunch by piling them onto a big crusty bun.

2 cups Barbecue Sauce (page 135), or store-bought vegan barbecue sauce
2 (8-ounce) packages tempeh, cut into 1-inch strips
1 tablespoon vegetable oil
3 garlic cloves, minced
1½ pounds collard greens (about 2 bunches), stemmed and chopped
¼ cup vegetable stock, or water
1 tablespoon low-sodium tamari, or soy sauce
2 teaspoons smoked paprika

1. Preheat the oven to 400°F. Have a medium baking dish ready.

2. Spread a little barbecue sauce on the bottom of the baking dish. Place the tempeh strips in the dish and cover them with the remaining sauce.

3. Bake for 20 minutes, flipping the tempeh strips after 10 minutes.

4. While the tempeh bakes, in large pot over medium-low heat, heat the vegetable oil. Add the garlic and cook for 1 to 2 minutes, or until fragrant.

5. Stir in the collard greens, vegetable stock, tamari, and paprika. Cover the pot and cook for 15 to 18 minutes, or until the greens are tender.

6. Serve the barbecue tempeh strips alongside the smoky greens.

First-Timer tip: If the tempeh tastes a little too fermented for your liking, simmer it in water or vegetable stock for 30 minutes before cutting it into strips.

Per serving: *Calories: 492; Fat: 17g; Carbohydrates: 67g; Fiber: 7g; Protein: 25g; Sodium: 1588mg; Iron: 4mg*

PORTOBELLO PEPPER STEAK WITH MASHED POTATOES

SERVES 4 / PREP TIME: 15 MINUTES / COOK TIME: 20 MINUTES

LEFTOVER-FRIENDLY • PLAN AHEAD

I never liked steak as a kid. I would eat my veggies and get stuck sitting at the table, not allowed to leave until I finished my meat. The one meaty dish I did like, though, was pepper steak, which I met in the form of those boil-in-a-bag meals that predated microwave dinners. Hearty portobellos take the place of meat here, but you can use seitan or store-bought vegan beef, too. I like to serve my pepper steak with mashed potatoes, because they soak up the sauce nicely, but rice is a great alternative.

3 pounds (about 9 medium) potatoes of choice, chopped

½ teaspoon salt, plus more for seasoning

2 teaspoons vegetable oil

1 small yellow onion, cut into slices

2 bell peppers, any color, seeded and cut into slices

4 large portobello mushrooms, stemmed and cut into slices

½ cup vegetable stock, or water

¼ cup low-sodium tamari, or soy sauce

1 tablespoon rice vinegar

1 tablespoon cornstarch

1 garlic clove, minced, or ¼ teaspoon garlic powder

½-inch piece fresh ginger, peeled and coarsely chopped, or ½ teaspoon ground ginger

½ teaspoon freshly ground black pepper, plus more for seasoning

½ cup Nut Milk of choice (page 130), or store-bought nondairy milk

1. In a large pot, combine the potatoes with enough water to cover them by 1 inch. Add the salt. Place the pot over high heat and bring the water to a boil. Cook for about 15 minutes until the potatoes are fork-tender.

2. While the potatoes cook, in a large pan over medium-high heat, heat the vegetable oil. Add the onion and cook for about 5 minutes, stirring frequently, until it begins to soften.

3. Add the bell peppers and mushrooms. Cook for about 10 minutes, stirring occasionally, until they soften.

Continued >

4. In a small bowl, whisk the vegetable stock, tamari, vinegar, cornstarch, garlic, ginger, and pepper to combine. Pour the mixture into the pan with the vegetables and gently stir to coat everything well. Cook for about 3 minutes until the sauce thickens and is heated through.

5. To make the mashed potatoes, drain the potatoes and place them back in the pot. Add the nut milk. Using a potato masher or fork, mash the potatoes until they reach your desired consistency. Season with salt and pepper.

6. Serve the pepper steak mixture over the mashed potatoes.

First-Timer tip: I like to leave the peels on my potatoes because they contain tons of nutrients, and because it saves time. You can mash pretty much any type of potato, but russet and Yukon mash up the fluffiest. Waxy potatoes are creamier, but if they're over-mashed, they may turn paste-like.

Per serving: *Calories: 325; Fat: 3g; Carbohydrates: 66g; Fiber: 11g; Protein: 11g; Sodium: 867mg; Iron: 3mg*

KUNG PAO SEITAN

SERVES 4 / PREP TIME: 15 MINUTES / COOK TIME: 20 MINUTES
LEFTOVER-FRIENDLY • PLAN AHEAD

When I get a hankering for something spicy—I'm talking sweaty forehead, watery eyes spicy—I head into the kitchen to cook up a spicy stir-fry. Why? Because stir-fries are easy and they can handle lots of spice. Go ahead and add extra veggies to this dish. . . I like to add broccoli or bok choy if I happen to have some in the refrigerator. If you're like me and don't mind (or actually relish) the heat, add more red pepper flakes. Throw in some dried spicy chiles, too, if you have them (and you're feeling brave).

2 teaspoons vegetable oil
1 pound Seitan (page 144), or store-bought seitan, cut into slices
10 ounces mushrooms, chopped (about 4 cups)
1 red bell pepper, seeded and chopped
8 ounces dried rice noodles, or soba noodles
1 cup vegetable stock, or water
¼ cup low-sodium tamari, or soy sauce
3 tablespoons rice vinegar
2 tablespoons cornstarch
½ teaspoon red pepper flakes
½ teaspoon freshly ground black pepper
¼ cup peanuts, chopped

1. In a large pan over medium-high heat, heat the vegetable oil. Add the seitan, mushrooms, and red bell pepper. Cook for 10 to 15 minutes, stirring frequently, until the veggies have softened and the seitan begins to brown.

2. While the vegetables and seitan cook, cook the noodles according to the package instructions.

3. In a small bowl, whisk the vegetable stock, tamari, vinegar, cornstarch, red pepper flakes, and black pepper. Pour the mixture into the pan with the seitan and vegetables. Stir to coat thoroughly and cook until the sauce thickens slightly and is heated through, about 5 minutes.

4. Serve the kung pao mixture over the noodles. Top with the chopped peanuts.

Per serving: Calories: 465; Fat: 9g; Carbohydrates: 59g; Fiber: 5g; Protein: 32g; Sodium: 1152mg; Iron: 3mg

SWEET AND SOUR TOFU

SERVES 4 / PREP TIME: 15 MINUTES / COOK TIME: 30 MINUTES
LEFTOVER-FRIENDLY • NUT-FREE • PLAN AHEAD

Ah, sweet and sour, my old take-out friend. It is possible to get vegan sweet and sour where I live, but the restaurant is just far enough away that they don't deliver, and it's quicker to make my own than it is to drive there and pick it up. Rather than spend time in a car, I prefer to be in my own home, cooking—and then immediately scarfing it down.

2 teaspoons vegetable oil, divided
3 tablespoons low-sodium tamari, or soy sauce, divided
3 tablespoons rice vinegar, or white wine vinegar, divided
1 (14-ounce) package extra-firm tofu, drained, pressed, and cubed (see page 15)
1 small sweet onion, chopped
1 red bell pepper, seeded and chopped
1 green bell pepper, seeded and chopped
1 cup canned diced pineapple, juice reserved
1 tablespoon tomato paste, or ketchup
2 tablespoons maple syrup
1 tablespoon cornstarch
4 cups cooked rice of choice (see page 14)

1. In a large pan over medium-high heat, heat 1 teaspoon of vegetable oil, 1 tablespoon of tamari, and 1 tablespoon of vinegar. Add the tofu and cook for about 10 minutes, stirring frequently, until it begins to brown on all sides. Transfer the tofu to a plate and cover to keep warm.

2. Add the remaining 1 teaspoon of vegetable oil to the pan along with the onion. Cook over medium-high heat for about 5 minutes, stirring frequently, until the onion begins to brown.

3. Add the red and green bell peppers and pineapple to the pan. Cook for about 10 more minutes, stirring occasionally, until the vegetables have softened. Add the tofu back to the pan.

Continued >

4. In a small bowl, whisk the tomato paste, maple syrup, cornstarch, remaining 2 tablespoons tamari, remaining 2 tablespoons of vinegar, and ½ cup of the reserved pineapple juice. Pour the sauce into the pan and gently stir to coat everything well. Cook for about 3 minutes until the sauce thickens and is heated through. Served over cooked rice.

First-Timer tip: If you're pressed for time, use store-bought baked tofu and a bag of frozen stir-fry vegetables in this recipe. Baked tofu is already seasoned, so you can skip step 1. Just add it to the pan with the frozen veggies in step 3. Cook until heated through, then add the sauce.

Per serving: *Calories: 426; Fat: 7g; Carbohydrates: 76g; Fiber: 3g; Protein: 14g; Sodium: 470mg; Iron: 5mg*

TEMPEH TERIYAKI

SERVES 4 / PREP TIME: 10 MINUTES / COOK TIME: 20 MINUTES

LEFTOVER-FRIENDLY • NUT-FREE • PLAN AHEAD

Teriyaki holds a special place in my heart. When I was little and my Poppop would come to visit, we'd go out to eat at a fancy restaurant and I'd always order teriyaki chicken and a Shirley Temple. It wasn't until I was older that I realized teriyaki was a sauce and not a type of chicken. Even though it's easy to make, it always seems like a special treat for me because it reminds me of those dinners with Poppop. The Shirley Temple is optional.

2 teaspoons vegetable oil

2 (8-ounce) packages tempeh, cubed

3 cups chopped broccoli florets (about 1 bunch broccoli)

½ cup low-sodium tamari, or soy sauce

¼ cup vegetable stock, or water

¼ cup rice vinegar

2 tablespoons cornstarch

1 tablespoon maple syrup

2 garlic cloves, minced, or ½ teaspoon garlic powder

1-inch piece fresh ginger, peeled and coarsely chopped, or 1 teaspoon ground ginger

4 cups cooked quinoa (see page 14)

1 tablespoon sesame seeds

1. In a large pan over medium-high heat, heat the vegetable oil. Add the tempeh and broccoli. Cook for 10 to 15 minutes, stirring frequently, until the broccoli has softened and the tempeh begins to brown.

2. In a small bowl, whisk the tamari, vegetable stock, vinegar, cornstarch, maple syrup, garlic, and ginger to combine. Pour the mixture into the pan. Stir to coat thoroughly and cook until the sauce has thickened slightly and heated through, about 5 minutes.

3. Serve the tempeh and broccoli over the cooked quinoa. Top with sesame seeds.

First-Timer tip: Don't feel like chopping broccoli? Add 2 (10-ounce) bags of frozen broccoli straight into the hot pan. No need to defrost it.

Per serving: *Calories: 583; Fat: 20g; Carbohydrates: 70g; Fiber: 8g; Protein: 34g; Sodium: 1115mg; Iron: 8mg*

CHICKPEA CURRY

SERVES 4 / PREP TIME: 15 MINUTES / COOK TIME: 20 MINUTES
GLUTEN-FREE • LEFTOVER-FRIENDLY • NUT-FREE • PLAN AHEAD

This recipe is based on the beloved Indian dish chana masala that I used to get at a delicious vegetarian Indian restaurant near me. Sadly, the restaurant moved, and I can no longer get my curry fix locally. I've done my best to recreate some of my favorites at home, and this chickpea dish is at the top of my most-loved list.

2 teaspoons vegetable oil
1 small yellow onion, chopped
2 (15-ounce) cans chickpeas, drained and rinsed, or 3 cups cooked chickpeas (see page 13)
1 (14-ounce) can diced tomatoes, drained
¼ cup vegetable stock, or water
3 garlic cloves, minced, or ½ teaspoon garlic powder
1-inch piece fresh ginger, peeled and coarsely chopped, or 1 teaspoon ground ginger
2 teaspoons curry powder
½ teaspoon ground turmeric
½ cup chopped fresh cilantro
1 tablespoon freshly squeezed lemon juice
Salt
Freshly ground black pepper
4 cups cooked rice of choice (see page 14)

1. In a large pan over medium-high heat, heat the vegetable oil. Add the onion and cook for about 5 minutes, stirring frequently, until it begins to brown.

2. Stir in the chickpeas, tomatoes, vegetable stock, garlic, ginger, curry powder, and turmeric. Bring the mixture to a boil and lower the heat to medium. Cook for 10 minutes, stirring occasionally, until most of the liquid has been absorbed.

3. Stir in the cilantro and lemon juice. Taste and season with salt and pepper. Serve the chickpea curry over the cooked rice.

First-Timer tip: Garbanzo beans and chickpeas are the same thing!

Per serving: *Calories: 494; Fat: 6g; Carbohydrates: 93g; Fiber: 11g; Protein: 17g; Sodium: 116mg; Iron: 6mg*

STUFFED PEPPERS

SERVES 4 / PREP TIME: 15 MINUTES / COOK TIME: 35 MINUTES
GLUTEN-FREE • LEFTOVER-FRIENDLY • NUT-FREE • PLAN AHEAD

The stuffed pepper is a thing of beauty. It's easy to make, but looks so pretty on a plate that people will think you've been toiling away in the kitchen for hours. Feel free to play with this recipe. You can swap out the lentils for another type of bean, or use cooked rice instead of quinoa. Pretty much any cooked veggie adds well to the mix, too. Serve the peppers with a little Tofu Sour Cream (page 132), if you like.

2 cups cooked quinoa (see page 14)
1 (15-ounce) can brown lentils, drained and rinsed, or 1½ cups cooked lentils (see
   page 12)
1 (14-ounce) can diced tomatoes, drained, liquid reserved
1 cup corn kernels, fresh or frozen and thawed
2 teaspoons chili powder
1 teaspoon garlic powder
½ teaspoon onion powder
¼ teaspoon salt
¼ teaspoon freshly ground black pepper
¼ teaspoon red pepper flakes (optional)
4 red bell peppers, halved, ribbed, and seeded

1. Preheat the oven to 375°F. Have a baking dish ready.

2. In large bowl, stir together the quinoa, lentils, tomatoes, corn, chili powder, garlic powder, onion powder, salt, pepper, and red pepper flakes (if using). Stuff the mix-ture into the bell pepper halves. Place the stuffed pepper halves in the baking dish and pour the reserved liquid from the tomatoes into the bottom of the dish. Cover the dish with aluminum foil.

3. Bake for 30 to 35 minutes, or until the peppers are tender and the filling is heated through. Serve with Tofu Sour Cream (page 132), if you like.

First-Timer tip: Removing the ribs and seeds from inside the peppers can be tricky. Use a paring knife or a spoon to scrape everything out. For a fancier presentation, cut the tops off the peppers and stuff them upright, then replace the tops like lids.

Per serving: *Calories: 339; Fat: 4g; Carbohydrates: 64g; Fiber: 14g; Protein: 16g; Sodium: 188mg; Iron: 10mg*

POKÉ BOWL

SERVES 4 / PREP TIME: 15 MINUTES, PLUS MARINATING TIME
LEFTOVER-FRIENDLY • PLAN AHEAD

Poké (pronounced *PO*-kay) is a Hawaiian dish of marinated raw tuna. It's usually served in a bowl over rice with vegetables—kind of a deconstructed sushi. This vegan version uses ginger-sesame marinated hearts of palm. If you miss the fishy flavor of traditional poké, throw in a little chopped nori seaweed.

1 tablespoon low-sodium tamari, or soy sauce
1 tablespoon freshly squeezed lime juice
1 teaspoon sesame oil
½-inch piece fresh ginger, peeled and coarsely chopped, or ½ teaspoon
    ground ginger
1 (14-ounce) can hearts of palm, drained and chopped
¼ cup Cashew Mayonnaise (page 131), or store-bought nondairy mayonnaise
¼ cup sriracha
4 cups cooked rice of choice (see page 14)
1 cup shelled edamame
2 carrots, grated
1 cucumber, chopped
1 avocado, peeled, halved, pitted, and chopped
2 scallions, sliced
2 tablespoons sesame seeds

1. In a small bowl, whisk the tamari, lime juice, sesame oil, and ginger to combine.

2. In a medium shallow bowl, combine the hearts of palm and dressing. Gently toss to coat and let marinate for about 15 minutes.

3. Meanwhile, in a small bowl, whisk the mayonnaise and sriracha to blend. Add a little water to thin it out if the sauce is too thick.

4. To assemble the poké bowls, place 1 cup of rice into a bowl and top it with some of the hearts of palm, ¼ cup of edamame, some carrot, cucumber, and avocado. Drizzle on the sriracha mayo and garnish with scallions and sesame seeds.

Per serving: Calories: 541; Fat: 18g; Carbohydrates: 84g; Fiber: 9g; Protein: 14g; Sodium: 809mg; Iron: 8mg

RED BEAN JAMBALAYA

SERVES 4 / PREP TIME: 15 MINUTES / COOK TIME: 40 MINUTES
GLUTEN-FREE • LEFTOVER-FRIENDLY • NUT-FREE

Jambalaya is a Creole-style rice dish made with meat and seafood, usually sausage and crawfish. I've seen recipes for jambalaya that have crazy-long lists of ingredients—about half of them spices. Listen, I love to cook, but I don't have time for that. When making jambalaya, I just use a Cajun (sometimes called Creole) spice blend.

2 teaspoons vegetable oil
2 green bell peppers, seeded and chopped
2 celery stalks, chopped
1 small yellow onion, chopped
3 garlic cloves, minced
2 (15-ounce) cans kidney beans, drained and rinsed, or 3 cups cooked kidney beans (see page 13)
1 (14-ounce) can diced tomatoes with their juices
2¼ cups vegetable stock, or water
1 cup uncooked white rice
2 tablespoons Cajun spice blend
Salt
Freshly ground black pepper
Hot sauce, for serving (optional)

1. In a large stockpot over medium-high heat, heat the vegetable oil. Add the green bell peppers, celery, onion, and garlic. Cook for about 10 minutes until the vegetables have softened.

2. Stir in the kidney beans, tomatoes and juice, vegetable stock, rice, and Cajun spice blend. Bring the mixture to a boil, then reduce the heat to medium-low. Cover the pot and simmer for 20 to 25 minutes, or until the rice has absorbed all the liquid.

3. Taste and season with salt and pepper. Serve with hot sauce (if using).

Substitution tip: If you prefer brown rice, it will take between 35 and 45 minutes for the rice to absorb the liquid in step 2.

Per serving: *Calories: 408; Fat: 3g; Carbohydrates: 78g; Fiber: 13g; Protein: 17g; Sodium: 199mg; Iron: 7mg*

MAC AND "CHEESE"

SERVES 6 / PREP TIME: 15 MINUTES / COOK TIME: 25 MINUTES
LEFTOVER-FRIENDLY

I don't think I've ever met anyone who doesn't love mac and cheese. I grew up on the boxed kind that's made with the powdery "cheese" mix—but always as a side dish. As an adult, I make the sauce with vegetables, and it's front and center on my plate.

2 waxy potatoes (such as red or new), peeled and chopped
2 carrots, chopped
1 garlic clove, peeled
½ cup raw cashews
12 ounces dried bite-size pasta, such as elbows, penne, or rotini
½ cup nutritional yeast
1 tablespoon freshly squeezed lemon juice
1 tablespoon cornstarch
1 teaspoon Dijon mustard
1 teaspoon salt

1. In a large pot, combine the potatoes, carrots, garlic, cashews, and enough water to cover the vegetables by 2 inches. Place the pot over medium-high heat and bring the water to a boil. Reduce the heat to medium and simmer for about 15 minutes, or until the vegetables are fork-tender. Drain, reserving 2 cups of the cooking water.

2. While the vegetables cook, cook the pasta according to the package instructions.

3. In a blender, combine the cooked vegetables, reserved cooking water, nutritional yeast, lemon juice, cornstarch, Dijon, and salt. Blend until smooth and creamy. Return the mixture to the pot, place it over medium-high heat, and bring to a boil. Reduce the heat and simmer for about 5 minutes until the sauce thickens slightly.

4. Pour the sauce over the cooked pasta and toss to coat well.

Variation tip: Turn the cheese sauce in this recipe into a spicy queso dip! Cut the measurements in half, then add 1 (14-ounce) can drained diced tomatoes, 1 teaspoon chili powder, ¼ teaspoon ground cumin, and a pinch of cayenne pepper to the mix before blending in.

Per serving: Calories: 403; Fat: 7g; Carbohydrates: 69g; Fiber: 10g; Protein: 21g; Sodium: 424mg; Iron: 4mg

PASTA CARBONARA

SERVES 6 / PREP TIME: 15 MINUTES / COOK TIME: 15 MINUTES
LEFTOVER-FRIENDLY • PLAN AHEAD

It's common to turn to pasta when first going vegan because it seems like a safe and easy bet. Not all pasta is vegan though, so check the ingredients list for eggs. Tomato is often the sauce of choice, but that can get boring after a while, so I like to mix things up with this creamy, tofu-based sauce. Pasta carbonara is traditionally made with bacon, but my vegan version uses smoky mushrooms. If mushrooms aren't your thing, use chopped, cooked, store-bought tempeh bacon or seitan bacon and skip the tamari and smoked paprika.

2 teaspoons vegetable oil
1 pound mushrooms, sliced
1 tablespoon low-sodium tamari, or soy sauce
1 teaspoon smoked paprika
1 teaspoon salt, divided
½ teaspoon freshly ground black pepper
½ cup peas, fresh or frozen and thawed
1 (12-ounce) package silken tofu
¼ cup vegetable stock, or water
2 tablespoons nutritional yeast
2 tablespoons freshly squeezed lemon juice
1 teaspoon onion powder
½ teaspoon garlic powder
12 ounces pasta of choice, cooked according to the package instructions
½ cup Almond Parmesan Crumbles (page 136), or store-bought nondairy parmesan

1. In a large pan over medium-high heat, heat the vegetable oil. Add the mushrooms, tamari, paprika, ½ teaspoon of salt, and the pepper. Cook for about 10 minutes, stirring frequently, until the mushrooms are soft and browned. Add the peas to the pan and cook for 2 or 3 minutes more.

2. While the mushrooms cook, in a blender, combine the tofu, vegetable stock, nutritional yeast, lemon juice, onion powder, garlic powder, and remaining ½ teaspoon of salt. Blend until smooth and creamy.

3. Place the pasta in a large bowl and add the tofu cream sauce. Toss to coat the pasta in the sauce. Gently toss in the mushrooms and peas, then stir in the almond parmesan crumbles.

Fun fact: *Carbonara* roughly translates to "in the manner of coal miners." It's believed that the dish was created so coal miners could have a hearty meal while they worked.

First-Timer tip: Carbonara is usually made with noodles, such as spaghetti or linguine, but just about any pasta shape will work. I like to use penne or rigatoni.

Per serving: *Calories: 352; Fat: 4g; Carbohydrates: 52g; Fiber: 4g; Protein: 24g; Sodium: 776mg; Iron: 3mg*

BAKED ZITI

SERVES 8 / PREP TIME: 15 MINUTES / COOK TIME: 40 MINUTES
LEFTOVER-FRIENDLY • PLAN AHEAD

Baked ziti is kind of like lasagna's lazy cousin. It has all the delicious, carb-tastic flavor with none of the fuss. Baked ziti is often made with sausage, but I use red lentils instead, as they're nice and meaty. They take about the same amount of time to boil as pasta, so I cook them right in the pot. Baked pasta tends to dry out, so be generous with your sauce.

1 pound dried ziti or penne
½ cup dried red lentils
1 (14-ounce) package firm tofu, pressed and drained (see page 15)
½ cup nutritional yeast
¼ cup freshly squeezed lemon juice
1 teaspoon dried basil
½ teaspoon garlic powder
½ teaspoon salt
2 (24-ounce) jars marinara sauce
1 cup Macadamia Mozzarella (page 139), sliced or shredded, or store-bought nondairy mozzarella
½ cup Almond Parmesan Crumbles (page 136), or store-bought nondairy parmesan

1. Preheat the oven to 375°F. Have a 9-by-12-inch baking dish or lasagna pan ready.

2. Bring a large pot of salted water to a boil over high heat. Add the pasta and lentils. Cook according to the package directions until the pasta is al dente—cooked through but slightly firm.

3. While the pasta cooks, crumble the tofu into a food processor and add the nutritional yeast, lemon juice, basil, garlic powder, and salt. Process for 2 to 3 minutes until the mixture looks like ricotta.

4. Drain the pasta and return it to the pot. Add one jar of marinara to the pot and stir to coat the pasta well. Gently fold in the tofu ricotta. You don't need to mix it well—leave big pockets of ricotta in places. Transfer the pasta to the baking dish.

5. Pour the remaining jar of sauce over the pasta, smoothing it out with the back of a wooden spoon or spatula. Cover the dish with aluminum foil.

6. Bake for 20 minutes.

7. Remove the foil from the pan. Spread the macadamia mozzarella over the ziti and sprinkle with the almond parmesan crumbles. Bake for 10 minutes more, uncovered, or until the cheese melts. Let cool for about 5 minutes before serving.

Variation tip: Add some healthy greens to your ziti! Toss 3 cups chopped Swiss chard, kale, or broccoli into the pasta pot about 3 minutes before the pasta is done. The hot water will cook the greens alongside the noodles.

Per serving: *Calories: 470; Fat: 7g; Carbohydrates: 71g; Fiber: 12g; Protein: 31g; Sodium: 1352mg; Iron: 4mg*

CHILI CORN BREAD CASSEROLE

SERVES 6 / PREP TIME: 15 MINUTES / COOK TIME: 25 MINUTES
LEFTOVER-FRIENDLY • NUT-FREE

Is there a more delicious pairing than chili and corn bread? Here, they're cooked together in one simple dish. This casserole couldn't be easier: Throw all the chili ingredients together and pour them into a baking dish. Then mix the corn bread ingredients and slap it on top. Pop it in the oven, put your feet up, and, before you know it, dinner is ready. Serve it with a generous spoonful of Tofu Sour Cream (page 132).

1 (15-ounce) can black beans, drained and rinsed, or 1½ cups cooked black beans (see page 13)
1 (15-ounce) can kidney beans, drained and rinsed, or 1½ cups cooked kidney beans (see page 13)
1 (15-ounce) can pinto beans, drained and rinsed, or 1½ cups cooked pinto beans (see page 13)
1 (28-ounce) can diced tomatoes with their juices
1 cup corn kernels, fresh or frozen and thawed
2 tablespoons chili powder
2 teaspoons ground cumin
1 teaspoon garlic powder
½ teaspoon onion powder
1 teaspoon salt, divided
¼ teaspoon freshly ground black pepper
1¼ cups soy milk
2 tablespoons apple cider vinegar
¼ cup vegetable oil
2 tablespoons maple syrup
1 cup cornmeal
1 cup all-purpose flour
2 teaspoons baking powder
½ teaspoon baking soda

1. Preheat the oven to 400°F. Have a 9-by-12-inch baking dish ready.

2. In a large bowl, stir together the black, kidney, and pinto beans, the tomatoes and their juice, the corn, chili powder, cumin, garlic powder, onion powder, ½ teaspoon of salt, and the pepper. Spread the mixture in your baking dish in an even layer.

3. In a small bowl, whisk the soy milk, vinegar, vegetable oil, and maple syrup to blend.

4. In a large bowl, stir together the cornmeal, flour, baking powder, baking soda, and the remaining ½ teaspoon of salt. Make a small well in the center of the dry ingredients and pour in the soy milk mixture. Gently stir to combine, being careful not to overmix the batter. Pour the batter over the chili, using the back of a wooden spoon or spatula to spread it evenly.

5. Bake for 20 to 25 minutes, or until a toothpick inserted in the center of the corn bread comes out clean. Let cool for about 5 minutes before serving.

Variation tip: If you'd like your chili to be a little more veggie-centric, add cooked onion and bell pepper. You can also add 1 cup of vegan burger crumbles for more of a stick-to-your-ribs dish.

Per serving: Calories: 534; Fat: 14g; Carbohydrates: 84g; Fiber: 16g; Protein: 21g; Sodium: 826mg; Iron: 7mg

CHAPTER 8

SOMETHING SWEET

I was an avid baker in my pre-vegan days, but after changing my diet, I was pretty much dessertless for a few years. How the heck does one bake without butter or eggs? After some trial and error (and a few pioneering cookbooks), I realized just how easy it is to do, and I was back in the kitchen whipping up batches of cookies and cupcakes. I'm sharing a few of my faves here, but be warned: These recipes skew toward indulgent rather than healthy, so put on your stretchy pants and treat yourself!

SNICKERDOODLE COOKIE DOUGH DIP

MAKES ABOUT 2 CUPS / PREP TIME: 10 MINUTES
GLUTEN-FREE • LEFTOVER-FRIENDLY • PLAN AHEAD

The first time someone offered me a snickerdoodle, I laughed, because I thought she had made up the word. I mean, it kind of sounds like one of those designer hybrid dogs, doesn't it? It turns out that snickerdoodles are delicious cinnamon sugar cookies. This dessert-style hummus dip is made with chickpeas, but has all the taste of a snickerdoodle and requires minimal effort. Serve it with sliced apples, pretzels, or pita chips for dipping.

1 (15-ounce) can chickpeas, drained and rinsed, or 1½ cups cooked chickpeas (see page 13)
¼ cup almond butter, or cashew butter
¼ cup maple syrup
2 tablespoons light brown sugar
2 tablespoons Nut Milk of choice (page 130), or store-bought nondairy milk, plus more as needed
2 teaspoons ground cinnamon
2 teaspoons vanilla extract

1. In a food processor, combine the chickpeas, almond butter, maple syrup, brown sugar, nut milk, cinnamon, and vanilla. Process until smooth and creamy. If the mixture seems too thick, add more nut milk, 1 tablespoon at a time, until the consistency is right.

2. Refrigerate in an airtight container for up to 1 week.

Variation tip: If chocolate is more your thing, skip the cinnamon and add ¼ cup unsweetened cocoa powder to the mixture. If you prefer peanut butter chocolate chip cookie dough dip, use ¼ cup peanut butter instead of almond butter and omit the cinnamon. Mix, then fold in ¼ cup nondairy chocolate chips.

Per serving (¼ cup): Calories: 140; Fat: 6g; Carbohydrates: 20g; Fiber: 3g; Protein: 4g; Sodium: 40mg; Iron: 1mg

PEANUT BUTTER TRUFFLES

MAKES 20 TRUFFLES / PREP TIME: 15 MINUTES / COOK TIME: 10 MINUTES

30 MINUTES OR LESS • GLUTEN-FREE • LEFTOVER-FRIENDLY

Hello, my name is Dianne and I'm a chocoholic. The only thing I like more than chocolate is the combination of chocolate and peanut butter. Rich, luxurious chocolate paired with creamy, peanut-y goodness—what's not to love? These little balls of melt-in-your-mouth deliciousness are so lush I only need one to satisfy a craving—although it's tempting to down a whole batch.

¾ cup rolled oats
1 cup (about 9) Medjool dates, pitted
1 cup creamy peanut butter
1 teaspoon vanilla extract
½ teaspoon salt
1¼ cups nondairy chocolate chips

1. Line a large baking sheet with parchment paper. Set aside.

2. In a food processor or blender, process the oats until they resemble flour.

3. Add the dates, peanut butter, vanilla, and salt. Process until the mixture resembles a smooth paste. Scoop out the mixture by tablespoons and roll into small balls, about 1½ inches in diameter. Place the balls on the prepared baking sheet.

4. Fill a small saucepan with water and place it over low heat. Put a slightly larger saucepan or stainless steel bowl on top. Add the chocolate chips to the top pan and heat, stirring constantly, until smooth and fully melted. Be careful not to burn the chocolate. Remove the chocolate from the heat as soon as it's melted.

5. Using a fork, dip each truffle into the melted chocolate, letting the excess drip back into the pan. Place the coated truffles back on the baking sheet.

6. Refrigerate the truffles to cool completely before serving. Keep refrigerated in an airtight container for 1 week.

First-Timer tip: If your dates seem a little tough, soak them in warm water for about 30 minutes before using them in this recipe. If you can't find Medjools, other date varieties are fine, but you'll need to soak them for about 2 hours before using them.

Per serving (1 truffle): *Calories: 252; Fat: 15g; Carbohydrates: 25g; Fiber: 5g; Protein: 6g; Sodium: 127mg; Iron: 3mg*

BLUEBERRY PEACH COBBLER

SERVES 6 / PREP TIME: 15 MINUTES / COOK TIME: 40 MINUTES

LEFTOVER-FRIENDLY • PLAN AHEAD

Cobblers, crisps, crumbles, buckles, Betties, slumps, and grunts—they're all baked fruit with some sort of topping. The difference comes down to exactly what that topping is. Cobblers have a biscuit-style topping. They work well with just about any type of fruit, so feel free to mix it up.

4 peaches, peeled, pitted, and cut into slices
3 cups fresh blueberries
¾ cup granulated sugar, divided
1 tablespoon cornstarch
1 tablespoon freshly squeezed lemon juice
1 teaspoon ground cinnamon, divided
1¼ cups all-purpose flour
1½ teaspoons baking powder
½ teaspoon salt
½ cup Nut Milk of choice (page 130), or store-bought nondairy milk
¼ cup vegetable oil
1 teaspoon vanilla extract

1. Preheat the oven to 375°F. Have an 8-by-11-inch baking pan ready.

2. In a large bowl, stir together the peaches, blueberries, ¼ cup of sugar, the cornstarch, lemon juice, and ½ teaspoon of cinnamon. Spread the fruit mixture into the bottom of the baking dish.

3. In another large bowl, whisk the flour, the remaining ½ cup of sugar, the baking powder, the remaining ½ teaspoon of cinnamon, and the salt to combine.

4. In a small bowl, stir together the nut milk, vegetable oil, and vanilla. Add the liquid ingredients to the flour mixture and stir until just combined. Do not overmix. Spread the topping over the fruit. It's okay if it's uneven.

5. Bake for 35 to 40 minutes, or until the fruit is bubbly and the topping is golden brown. Let cool slightly before serving.

Per serving: Calories: 375; Fat: 10g; Carbohydrates: 70g; Fiber: 4g; Protein: 5g; Sodium: 212mg; Iron: 3mg

APPLE GALETTE

SERVES 8 / PREP TIME: 15 MINUTES / COOK TIME: 45 MINUTES
LEFTOVER-FRIENDLY • NUT-FREE • PLAN AHEAD

A galette is a flat, round French pastry, similar to a pie or tart. You'll often hear the word "rustic" used to describe it, because "messy" sounds a little impolite. It's messy in a good way, though, because a galette is essentially a pie made without a pie dish. It's easier to make than a traditional pie, too—no need to worry about crust crimping or latticework. I've seen really pretty galettes with the fruit filling fanned out into fancy patterns, but it tastes the same if you just pile it on and bake it up.

1 recipe Pastry Dough (page 141), chilled, or 12 ounces store-bought vegan
   pastry dough
1½ pounds apples, cored and thinly sliced
¼ cup packed light brown sugar
1 tablespoon freshly squeezed lemon juice
1 teaspoon ground cinnamon
¼ teaspoon salt
1 tablespoon olive oil
1 teaspoon granulated sugar

1. Preheat the oven to 400°F. Have a large baking sheet ready.

2. Place the dough on a piece of parchment paper and cover it with another piece of parchment. Using a rolling pin, roll the dough into a large circle, about ⅛ inch thick and 14 inches in diameter. Remove the top layer of parchment. Carefully lift the dough by the bottom piece of parchment and transfer it to the baking sheet with the paper.

3. In a large bowl, combine the apple slices, brown sugar, lemon juice, cinnamon, and salt. Gently toss to coat the apples. Arrange the apple slices on the pastry, leaving a 2-inch border. It's okay if the slices overlap.

4. Gently fold the edges of the dough up over the apple slices, pleating it if necessary. If the dough cracks, pinch it back together.

5. Brush the edges of the dough with the olive oil and sprinkle them with the granulated sugar.

6. Bake for 40 to 45 minutes, or until the crust is golden brown and the apples are tender. Let cool completely before slicing and serving.

First-Timer tip: Just about any type of apple will work for this, but the best baking apples are Pink Lady, Honey Crisp, Jonagold, Braeburn, and Granny Smith.

Substitution tip: Sliced Bartlett pears also work really well in this recipe. Try them on their own or do a mixture of pears and apples.

Per serving: *Calories: 215; Fat: 7g; Carbohydrates: 39g; Fiber: 5g; Protein: 1g; Sodium: 179mg; Iron: 1mg*

CHOCOLATE CHIP COOKIES

MAKES 36 COOKIES / PREP TIME: 15 MINUTES / COOK TIME: 15 MINUTES
LEFTOVER-FRIENDLY • PLAN AHEAD

Growing up, baking cookies meant slicing one of those logs of refrigerated dough, plopping it on a baking sheet, and sliding it into the oven. The best part of making cookies back then was eating the dough straight from the package, which I now know is a no-no. Not only are raw eggs unsafe, raw flour can harbor bacteria. These cookies take slightly more effort than those treats from my childhood—but not much.

2½ cups all-purpose flour
1 teaspoon baking powder
1 teaspoon baking soda
1 teaspoon salt
¾ cup granulated sugar
¾ cup packed light brown sugar
½ cup vegetable oil
¾ cup Nut Milk of choice (page 130), or store-bought nondairy milk
2 teaspoons vanilla extract
1½ cups nondairy chocolate chips

1. Preheat the oven to 350°F. Line two baking sheets with parchment paper. Set aside.

2. In a medium bowl, whisk the flour, baking powder, baking soda, and salt to combine.

3. In a large bowl, stir together the granulated sugar, brown sugar, vegetable oil, nut milk, and vanilla. Add the flour mixture to the sugar mixture and stir until just combined. Do not overmix. Fold in the chocolate chips. Scoop the dough by tablespoons onto the prepared baking sheets, about 2 inches apart.

4. Bake for 12 to 15 minutes, or until the edges are golden brown.

5. Let cool for 2 minutes, then transfer the cookies to a wire rack to cool completely. Store leftovers in an airtight container.

First-Timer tip: When buying chocolate chips, check the ingredients list for milk or milk fat. (Cocoa butter comes from cacao beans, so it's safe for vegans to eat.) I like the brands Enjoy Life and Equal Exchange.

Per serving (1 cookie): *Calories: 159; Fat: 9g; Carbohydrates: 17g; Fiber: 2g; Protein: 2g; Sodium: 113mg; Iron: 1mg*

CHOCOLATE CREAM PIE

SERVES 8 / PREP TIME: 10 MINUTES, PLUS CHILLING TIME
LEFTOVER-FRIENDLY • PLAN AHEAD

Most families have traditions of serving pumpkin or apple pie for holiday desserts. Mine had chocolate cream pie, and I was usually the one who made it. I found an easy recipe in a magazine that used a store-bought piecrust, melted chocolate, and premade whipped topping. It took me about 5 minutes to make, and everyone loved it. This recipe is just as easy. It requires just five ingredients, a few minutes, and a whole lot of love. Not in the mood for pie? Skip the crust and serve the filling as a pudding.

2 cups nondairy chocolate chips
1 (12-ounce) package silken tofu
½ cup full-fat coconut milk
½ cup maple syrup
1 recipe Pastry Dough, blind baked (page 141), or store-bought piecrust prepared
   according to the package instructions

1. Fill a small saucepan with water and place it over low heat. Place a slighter larger saucepan or stainless steel bowl on top. Add the chocolate chips to the top bowl and heat, stirring constantly, until smooth and fully melted. Be careful not to burn the chocolate. Transfer the melted chocolate to a food processor or blender.

2. Add the tofu, coconut milk, and maple syrup. Blend until smooth and creamy. Pour the mixture into the prepared piecrust.

3. Refrigerate the pie for 2 to 4 hours until the filling is set. Enjoy!

Substitution tip: Try your favorite nut butter or sun butter in place of the coconut milk for a peanut butter cup pie.

Per serving: *Calories: 359; Fat: 27g; Carbohydrates: 33g; Fiber: 6g; Protein: 8g; Sodium: 129mg; Iron: 6mg*

LEMON BARS

SERVES 9 / PREP TIME: 10 MINUTES / COOK TIME: 50 MINUTES
LEFTOVER-FRIENDLY • PLAN AHEAD

When it comes to dessert, I usually go for something chocolaty or nutty (or chocolaty *and* nutty). However, I'm always pleasantly surprised by how much I like lemon bars. With a bright and tangy lemon cream sitting on top of a cookie-like crust, it's a whole lot of yum. If you prefer lime to lemon, substitute key lime juice and zest.

1½ cups all-purpose flour
1 cup granulated sugar, divided
½ teaspoon salt
½ cup Nut Milk of choice (page 130), or store-bought nondairy milk
½ cup coconut oil, at room temperature
1 (12-ounce) package silken tofu
½ cup freshly squeezed lemon juice
¼ cup cornstarch
1 teaspoon grated lemon zest
Powdered sugar, for dusting

1. Preheat the oven to 350°F. Line an 8-by-8-inch baking pan with parchment paper.

2. In a medium bowl, stir together the flour, ¼ cup of sugar, and salt to combine.

3. Stir in the nut milk and coconut oil until just combined. It's okay if the dough is a little crumbly. Press the dough into the prepared baking pan.

4. Bake for 20 minutes, or until the crust is golden brown.

5. While the crust bakes, in a blender or food processor, combine the remaining ¾ cup of sugar, the silken tofu, lemon juice, cornstarch, and lemon zest. Process until smooth and creamy. Pour the filling on top of the baked crust.

6. Bake the lemon bars for 25 to 30 minutes, or until the filling is firm. Let cool for 10 minutes, then refrigerate for 2 hours to cool completely before dusting with powdered sugar, slicing, and serving.

First-Timer tip: Unrefined coconut oil will give your bars a slightly coconut-y taste. However, refined coconut oil doesn't taste like coconut.

Per serving: *Calories: 315; Fat: 14g; Carbohydrates: 45g; Fiber: 1g; Protein: 5g; Sodium: 155mg; Iron: 2mg*

CARROT CAKE CUPCAKES

MAKES 12 CUPCAKES / PREP TIME: 15 MINUTES / COOK TIME: 25 MINUTES
LEFTOVER-FRIENDLY • PLAN AHEAD

In an office where I once worked, I was known as the workplace weirdo because of my diet. Coworkers would sometimes make jokes about me sitting at my desk snacking on bean sprouts. (I don't know a single vegan who snacks on bean sprouts.) When I got a new job, I wanted to start on a good food foot, so I began baking cupcakes for holidays and birthdays. My coworkers gobbled them up, all but inventing holidays so there would be an excuse for me to bake. A workplace weirdo no more, I was soon crowned the Cupcake Queen, monarch of all things sugary.

⅔ cup soy milk
½ cup applesauce
1 tablespoon apple cider vinegar
2 teaspoons vanilla extract, divided
1½ cups all-purpose flour
¾ cup granulated sugar
1 teaspoon ground cinnamon
1 teaspoon baking soda
1 teaspoon baking powder
½ teaspoon salt
1 cup grated carrot
¼ cup raisins
¼ cup chopped walnuts
¼ cup Cashew Cream Cheese (page 138), or store-bought nondairy cream cheese
¼ cup refined coconut oil, slightly softened
2 cups confectioners' sugar

1. Preheat the oven to 350°F. Line a 12-cup muffin tin (or two 6-cup tins) with paper liners. Set aside.

2. In a medium bowl, stir together the soy milk, applesauce, vinegar, and 1 teaspoon of vanilla.

3. In a large bowl, whisk the flour, granulated sugar, cinnamon, baking soda, baking powder, and salt to combine. Pour the wet ingredients into the dry ingredients and stir until just combined. Don't overmix. Carefully fold in the carrot, raisins, and walnuts. Scoop the batter into the prepared muffin tin, filling each liner about two-thirds full.

4. Bake for 20 to 25 minutes, or until a toothpick inserted into the center of a cupcake comes out clean.

5. While the cupcakes bake, make the frosting. In a large bowl, combine the cashew cream cheese, coconut oil, and the remaining teaspoon of vanilla. Using a handheld electric mixer, beat to combine.

6. Slowly add the confectioners' sugar, ½ cup at a time. Beat until soft and fluffy.

7. Let the cupcakes cool completely before topping them with the cream cheese frosting.

First-Timer tip: Not all granulated sugar is vegan. Some sugars are filtered through charred animal bones to decolorize them and remove impurities. If the sugar is really white, chances are it's bone char sugar. Most organic sugars aren't filtered this way. Look for organic coconut sugar, raw sugar, or evaporated cane juice. Some brands even state they're vegan on the package.

Per serving: *Calories: 280; Fat: 8g; Carbohydrates: 50g; Fiber: 2g; Protein: 3g; Sodium: 234mg; Iron: 1mg*

CHAPTER 9

HOMEMADE ESSENTIALS

It's an amazing time to be vegan, because it's easier than ever to find vegan essentials in just about any grocery store. It hasn't always been this way, though. Back in the early days, dairy-free salad dressings and sour cream were difficult to come by, and when they were available, they were often inedible. So, I got crafty and made my own staples with ingredients like nuts and tofu. I still make my own rather than buying them at the store—not only does it save money, it's healthier because I know exactly what's going into them. Feel free to customize any of these recipes to your liking or food sensitivities.

NUT MILK

MAKES ABOUT 4 CUPS / PREP TIME: 5 MINUTES, PLUS SOAKING TIME
GLUTEN-FREE • LEFTOVER-FRIENDLY • PLAN AHEAD

Store-bought nut milks are convenient, but they sometimes contain questionable ingredients. What the heck is sunflower lectin? Does locust bean gum come from bugs? (It doesn't.) Making your own at home is easy with just a few ingredients, and it's customizable. Give it a hint of vanilla or, if you prefer your milk on the sweeter side, agave or maple syrup. Make sure your nuts are raw, as this recipe won't work if they're roasted or salted. Don't skimp on the soaking time, either. Soaking nut softens them, making them easier to blend.

1 cup raw nuts, such as almonds, cashews, or macadamias, soaked in water, drained, and rinsed (see page 15)
4 cups filtered water
¼ teaspoon salt
1 teaspoon vanilla extract (optional)
1 to 2 tablespoons agave nectar, or maple syrup (optional)

1. In a blender, combine the soaked nuts, water, salt, vanilla (if using), and agave (if using). Blend on high speed until the nuts are broken down into a very fine meal and the water is white and opaque. This might take 2 to 3 minutes.

2. Line a fine-mesh strainer with 2 layers of cheesecloth and place it over a large bowl. Pour the nut milk through the strainer. Gather the ends of the cheesecloth and twist them closed. Using your hands, squeeze the pulp in the cheesecloth, extracting as much milk as possible.

3. Refrigerate the nut milk in a sealed container for up to 4 days.

First-Timer tip: Don't throw away that leftover pulp! Add it to foods like smoothies and oatmeal or fold it into Apple Cinnamon Granola (page 31) before baking. Not sure what to do with it yet? Freeze the leftover pulp until you're ready to use it.

Per serving (1 cup): *Calories: 40; Fat: 3g; Carbohydrates: 2g; Fiber: 0g; Protein: 1g; Sodium: 180mg; Iron: 0mg*

CASHEW MAYONNAISE

MAKES ABOUT 1 CUP / PREP TIME: 5 MINUTES, PLUS SOAKING TIME
GLUTEN-FREE • LEFTOVER-FRIENDLY • PLAN AHEAD

When I first changed my diet, there was one brand of vegan mayo on the market and it wasn't very good. Still, I would buy it and force myself to use it, because what else was I going to use to make Chickpea Salad Sandwiches (page 73)? But then I discovered the magic of blended cashews, and everything changed. I started whipping up batches of homemade mayo and slathering it all over sandwiches and wraps. There are many more brands of vegan mayonnaise available now, and they're all pretty tasty, but most are loaded with oil. I don't follow an oil-free diet, but I don't want *that* much of it in my meals, so I still like to make my own.

¾ cup raw cashews, soaked in water, drained, and rinsed (see page 15)
⅓ cup filtered water, plus more as needed
2 tablespoons freshly squeezed lemon juice
1 tablespoon apple cider vinegar
1 teaspoon Dijon mustard
½ teaspoon garlic powder
½ teaspoon salt

1. In a blender, combine the soaked cashews, water, lemon juice, vinegar, Dijon, garlic powder, and salt. Blend on high speed until smooth and creamy. If the mayo is too thick, add more water, 1 tablespoon at a time, until it reaches your desired consistency.
2. Refrigerate the mayonnaise in an airtight container for up to 1 week.

Substitution tip: Use soaked blanched almonds or raw macadamia nuts instead of cashews. If you're allergic to nuts, substitute 1 cup silken tofu for the cashews.

Per serving (1 tablespoon): *Calories: 34; Fat: 3g; Carbohydrates: 2g; Fiber: 0g; Protein: 1g; Sodium: 78mg; Iron: 0mg*

TOFU SOUR CREAM

MAKES ABOUT 1½ CUPS / PREP TIME: 5 MINUTES
30 MINUTES OR LESS • GLUTEN-FREE • LEFTOVER-FRIENDLY • NUT-FREE

I can't think of any savory dish that doesn't taste a little better with sour cream. If you have the ingredients on hand, you can mix up a batch in less time than it would take to drive to the store to pick up a container. Drizzle it onto your tacos and burritos, add a dollop to a baked potato, or swirl a spoonful into soups. It's great in dips, too.

1 (12-ounce) package silken tofu
2 tablespoons freshly squeezed lime juice
1 tablespoon apple cider vinegar
½ teaspoon salt

1. In a blender, combine the tofu, lime juice, vinegar, and salt. Blend until smooth and creamy.
2. Refrigerate the sour cream in an airtight container for up to 1 week.

First-Timer tip: When buying silken tofu, look for the type in the shelf-stable carton (it doesn't need to be refrigerated).

Substitution tip: Use soaked raw nuts in the place of tofu if you like. Try ¾ cup cashews, almonds, or macadamias. See the soaking instructions on page 15.

Per serving (2 tablespoons): *Calories: 19; Fat: 1g; Carbohydrates: 1g; Fiber: 0g; Protein: 2g; Sodium: 107mg; Iron: 0mg*

TOFU RANCH DRESSING

MAKES ABOUT 1 CUP / PREP TIME: 5 MINUTES

30 MINUTES OR LESS • GLUTEN-FREE • LEFTOVER-FRIENDLY • NUT-FREE

I'm not sure how it happened, but ranch dressing seems to have snuck into my kitchen and taken over the condiment rack. Who needs ketchup and mustard when you have cool ranch? With its fresh, tangy flavor and creamy texture, it's an ideal complement to most savory dishes. In addition to being a terrific dressing for salads and a dip for cut veggies, it's great on sandwiches, wraps, and burgers. Actually, my advice is to pour it over anything.

1 cup silken tofu
1 tablespoon freshly squeezed lemon juice
1 tablespoon apple cider vinegar
1 garlic clove, minced
2 teaspoons chopped fresh parsley
½ teaspoon dried dill
½ teaspoon onion powder
½ teaspoon garlic powder
½ teaspoon salt

1. In a blender, combine the tofu, lemon juice, vinegar, garlic, parsley, dill, onion powder, garlic powder, and salt. Blend until smooth and creamy.

2. Refrigerate in an airtight container for up to 1 week.

Substitution tip: If you'd prefer cashew ranch, use ¾ cup soaked cashews and ¼ cup water instead of the silken tofu. See the soaking instructions on page 15.

Fun fact: Ranch dressing was developed by California dude ranch owner Steve Henson. The ranch's customers enjoyed it so much he began selling it for them to take home. The dressing became so popular he eventually opened a factory to manufacture it.

Per serving (2 tablespoons): *Calories: 23; Fat: 1g; Carbohydrates: 1g; Fiber: 0g; Protein: 2g; Sodium: 160mg; Iron: 0mg*

BARBECUE SAUCE

MAKES ABOUT 1¼ CUPS / PREP TIME: 10 MINUTES / COOK TIME: 15 MINUTES
30 MINUTES OR LESS · GLUTEN-FREE · LEFTOVER-FRIENDLY · NUT-FREE

Different regions of the United States have their own versions of barbecue sauce, but most start with a base of tomatoes, vinegar, and spices. I'm from New Jersey and—full disclosure—we don't know much about barbecue sauce in our neck of the woods. We like to cook with it, but we don't know anything about making it. This is my own take on various sauces I've tried and liked. Use it as a condiment on burgers or sandwiches, as a marinade for tofu and tempeh, or as a dipping sauce for roasted veggies or fries.

1 cup ketchup
3 tablespoons molasses
2 tablespoons yellow mustard
2 tablespoons apple cider vinegar
1 teaspoon low-sodium tamari, or soy sauce
½ teaspoon onion powder
½ teaspoon garlic powder
¼ teaspoon salt
¼ teaspoon cayenne pepper (optional)

1. In a medium saucepan over medium-high heat, stir together the ketchup, molasses, mustard, vinegar, tamari, onion powder, garlic powder, salt, and cayenne (if using). Bring to a boil, then reduce the heat to medium-low and simmer, uncovered, for about 10 minutes, or until the sauce thickens slightly.

2. Use the sauce immediately or let cool and refrigerate it in an airtight container for up to 2 weeks.

Variation tip: Change the flavor of your barbecue sauce by adding different ingredients. For a spicy sauce, add 2 to 3 tablespoons of your favorite hot sauce. For a fruity barbecue sauce, add 1 cup of peeled, chopped fruit—such as peaches, plums, apricots, or mangoes—to the saucepan. Allow the sauce to cool and then purée it in a blender. If you like a smoky sauce, add a dash of liquid smoke or a pinch of smoked paprika.

Per serving: *Calories: 37; Fat: 0g; Carbohydrates: 9g; Fiber: 0g; Protein: 1g; Sodium: 319mg; Iron: 0mg*

ALMOND PARMESAN CRUMBLES

MAKES ABOUT 1 CUP / PREP TIME: 5 MINUTES

30 MINUTES OR LESS • **GLUTEN-FREE** • **LEFTOVER-FRIENDLY**

I pour, rather than sprinkle, these noochy crumbles on pretty much everything. I love them on pasta, popcorn, salads, and even Loaded Avocado Toast (page 29) and Veggie-Loaded Tofu Scramble (page 32). You can use any kind of nut or seed in this recipe—each will give it a slightly different flavor profile. Be careful not to overprocess your crumbles or you'll end up with a cheese-flavored nut butter! (It'll still be delicious, but not what you're going for with this recipe.)

½ cup raw almonds
½ cup nutritional yeast
½ teaspoon dried mustard
½ teaspoon garlic powder
½ teaspoon salt

1. In a spice grinder or small food processor, pulse the almonds until they're finely ground.
2. Add the nutritional yeast, dried mustard, garlic powder, and salt. Pulse to incorporate.
3. Refrigerate in an airtight container for up to 1 month.

First-Timer tip: If you have almond flour on hand, skip the food processor and make this recipe the lazy way. Just toss ½ cup almond flour in a jar with the nutritional yeast and spices, make sure the lid is on tight, and give it a good shake.

Per serving (2 tablespoons): *Calories: 100; Fat: 4g; Carbohydrates: 9g; Fiber: 5g; Protein: 10g; Sodium: 152mg; Iron: 1mg*

TOFU FETA

MAKES ABOUT 2 CUPS / PREP TIME: 10 MINUTES, PLUS MARINATING TIME
GLUTEN-FREE • LEFTOVER-FRIENDLY • NUT-FREE

Growing up, cheese meant Cheddar, American, and that weird orange spray-can goo. I didn't discover feta until my adult years, and I only grew to really love it in the last of my pre-vegan days, right before I gave up dairy. Although there are lots of premade vegan cheeses available, I haven't been able to find a nondairy feta I love as much as the original. So, I started to make my own using tofu. It's not exactly like the real thing, but it's a close second. Toss it into salads or wraps—even use it as a pizza topping.

1 (14-ounce) package extra-firm tofu, drained and pressed (see page 15)
¼ cup freshly squeezed lemon juice
¼ cup apple cider vinegar
2 tablespoons nutritional yeast
1 teaspoon dried oregano
½ teaspoon garlic powder
½ teaspoon salt

1. Crumble the tofu into large chunks and place it into a shallow dish.
2. In a small bowl, whisk the lemon juice, vinegar, nutritional yeast, oregano, garlic powder, and salt to combine. Pour the mixture over the tofu and gently toss to combine.
3. Refrigerate the tofu for 2 to 4 hours to soak up the marinade.

First-Timer tip: The longer the tofu sits in the marinade, the stronger the flavor will be. Refrigerate any leftover tofu in the marinade, covered, for 3 to 5 days.

Per serving (2 tablespoons): *Calories: 36; Fat: 2g; Carbohydrates: 1g; Fiber: 1g; Protein: 4g; Sodium: 81mg; Iron: 0mg*

CASHEW CREAM CHEESE

MAKES ABOUT 1½ CUPS / PREP TIME: 15 MINUTES, PLUS SOAKING AND CHILLING TIME
GLUTEN-FREE • LEFTOVER-FRIENDLY • PLAN AHEAD

One of my biggest weaknesses is a big, fluffy whole-wheat everything bagel with a generous schmear of herbed cream cheese. Cream cheese is not just for bagels, though. Try it on toast, crackers, or muffins. You can swirl it into soups, make dips with it, and even use it as a pastry filling. This recipe is freezer-friendly, so make an extra batch and pop half in the freezer for those days when a craving strikes.

1 cup raw cashews, soaked in water, drained, and rinsed (see page 15)
3 to 4 tablespoons filtered water, plus more as needed
1 tablespoon nutritional yeast
1 tablespoon freshly squeezed lemon juice
1 tablespoon apple cider vinegar
½ teaspoon salt

1. In a food processor or blender, combine the soaked cashews, water, nutritional yeast, lemon juice, vinegar, and salt. Process until smooth and creamy. You may need to stop occasionally to scrape down the sides. If the mixture is too thick, add more filtered water, 1 teaspoon at a time, until the consistency is right.

2. Refrigerate the cream cheese in an airtight container for 1 to 2 hours before serving to firm it up.

3. Keep refrigerated in an airtight container for up to 1 week.

Variation tip: For scallion cream cheese, stir in ¼ cup sliced scallion. For herbed cream cheese, stir in 1 garlic clove, minced, 2 tablespoons chopped fresh dill, 2 tablespoons chopped fresh chives, and 2 tablespoons chopped fresh parsley. For vegetable cream cheese, stir in ¼ cup finely chopped carrot, ¼ cup finely chopped red bell pepper, 2 tablespoons sliced scallion, and 2 tablespoons chopped fresh parsley.

Per serving (2 tablespoons): *Calories: 64; Fat: 5g; Carbohydrates: 4g; Fiber: 1g; Protein: 3g; Sodium: 99mg; Iron: 0mg*

MACADAMIA MOZZARELLA

MAKES ABOUT 1 CUP / PREP TIME: 10 MINUTES, PLUS SOAKING AND COOLING TIME /
COOK TIME: 10 MINUTES

GLUTEN-FREE • LEFTOVER-FRIENDLY • PLAN AHEAD

Somer McCowan perfected the art of homemade, melty, nondairy mozzarella on her blog *Vedged Out* several years ago using cashews and tapioca starch. I think of her as a pioneer in the vegan cheese world, toiling away over vats of blended nuts, searching for melty perfection. Tapioca starch, also known as tapioca flour, may seem like a foreign ingredient, but you can usually find it in the baking aisle of the grocery store. It's the key to stretchy, melty cheese, so don't skip it. This cheese is similar to fresh mozzarella in that it will stay soft. It can be grated, but it works best sliced or even just dolloped in chunks.

½ cup unsalted macadamia nuts, soaked in water, drained, and rinsed (see page 15)
½ cup filtered water
¼ cup tapioca starch
2 tablespoons nutritional yeast
1 tablespoon freshly squeezed lemon juice
1 teaspoon white miso
½ teaspoon garlic powder
½ teaspoon salt

1. In a blender, combine the soaked macadamias, water, tapioca starch, nutritional yeast, lemon juice, miso, garlic powder, and salt. Blend until smooth and creamy.

2. Transfer the mixture to a medium saucepan and place it over medium heat. Cook for about 10 minutes, whisking constantly, until the mixture is stretchy and begins to form into a ball. It may get lumpy before it smooths out—keep whisking if it does.

3. Transfer the mixture to a container and cool in the refrigerator for 1 to 2 hours before using.

4. Keep refrigerated in an airtight container for 2 to 3 days.

Substitution tip: Swap the macadamias for soaked blanched almonds or raw cashews if you like. See the soaking instructions on page 15.

Per serving (¼ cup): *Calories: 184; Fat: 13g; Carbohydrates: 15g; Fiber: 4g; Protein: 5g; Sodium: 337mg; Iron: 1mg*

PASTRY DOUGH

MAKES 1 PIECRUST (ABOUT 12 OUNCES) / PREP TIME: 15 MINUTES, PLUS CHILLING TIME /
COOK TIME: 45 MINUTES (FOR A FINISHED PIE)

NUT-FREE • PLAN AHEAD

I used to get lazy when making pies and go for those store-bought, premade crusts. It's actually easy to make dough at home, though, and once I got the hang of it, I realized the error of my ways. In addition to baking pies with it, you can use pastry dough to make mini tarts, turnovers, cinnamon twists, crackers, and sandwich cookies. I suggest leaving out the maple syrup if you plan to use this dough in a savory recipe, unless you don't mind a hint of sweetness.

1½ cups all-purpose flour
½ teaspoon salt
¼ cup ice-cold olive oil, plus more for the pie pan
2 tablespoons maple syrup
2 to 4 tablespoons ice water

1. In a large bowl, mix the flour and salt. Drizzle the olive oil into the bowl and use a rubber spatula or wooden spoon to stir it into the flour. Mix until the flour resembles pebbles.

2. Drizzle the maple syrup and 2 tablespoons of ice water into the bowl and mix lightly until the mixture forms a dough. You may need to use your hands to knead the mixture a little until it becomes a stiff dough. If the mixture seems too dry, add more ice water, 1 tablespoon at a time. Form the dough into a ball, wrap it in plastic wrap, and refrigerate it for 2 hours.

3. To make a pie, preheat the oven to 375°F. Lightly coat a 9-inch pie pan with olive oil.

4. Place the dough on a piece of parchment paper and cover it with another piece of parchment. Using a rolling pin, roll out the dough from the center until it's about ¼ inch thick. Carefully transfer the dough to the prepared pie pan. Trim any dough that's hanging over the edge of the pan and crimp the dough edges using a fork or your fingers.

5. Fill with your favorite fillings. Bake for 30 to 40 minutes, or until the crust is golden brown and the filling is heated through.

Continued >

6. To blind bake your crust (that is, to bake it without a filling), place a piece of parchment paper inside the crust and fill it with pie weights or dried beans, then bake it for 15 minutes. Remove the crust from the oven and remove the parchment paper and pie weights. Prick the bottom of the crust a few times with a fork, then return it to the oven for another 15 to 20 minutes, or until it's golden brown.

First-Timer tip: Place your oil in the freezer about 30 minutes before you're going to make the recipe so it thickens.

Per serving (⅛ crust): *Calories: 169; Fat: 7g; Carbohydrates: 23g; Fiber: 1g; Protein: 3g; Sodium: 118mg; Iron: 1mg*

PIZZA DOUGH

MAKES 1 (16-INCH) PIZZA CRUST / PREP TIME: 15 MINUTES, PLUS RESTING TIME /
COOK TIME: 12 MINUTES (FOR A FINISHED PIZZA)

NUT-FREE • PLAN AHEAD

Making your own dough is fun—like a grown-up, edible version of Play-Doh. I've had people ask me if yeast is vegan, because it bubbles and grows and seems to be alive. It's a single-cell organism classified as a fungus, in the same family as mushrooms. So yes, it's totally vegan. In addition to pizza crust, you can use this dough to make Spinach Mushroom Calzones (page 90).

1 cup warm water
1 (0.25-ounce) package active dry yeast
1 teaspoon sugar
2½ cups all-purpose flour, plus more as needed
2 tablespoons olive oil
1 teaspoon salt

1. In a medium bowl, whisk the water, yeast, and sugar. Let the mixture stand until the yeast dissolves, about 5 minutes.

2. Add the flour, olive oil, and salt to the mixture and mix until a dough forms. Cover the bowl with a clean kitchen towel and let sit in a draft-free area for about 1 hour, or until the dough doubles in size.

3. To make a pizza, preheat the oven to 450°F. Lightly flour a 16-inch pizza pan and your work surface.

4. With a rolling pin, roll the dough on the prepared surface until it's 15 to 16 inches in diameter. Transfer it to your prepared pizza pan. If you don't have a rolling pin, use your hands to carefully stretch the dough right on the pizza pan.

5. Cover the dough with your favorite toppings. Bake for 10 to 12 minutes, or until the crust turns golden brown and the toppings are hot.

First-Timer tip: Once the dough has doubled in size, you can refrigerate it in an airtight container for up to 2 weeks, or freeze for up to 3 months. Before making your pizza, bring the dough to room temperature on the countertop.

Per serving (⅛ pizza): *Calories: 194; Fat: 4g; Carbohydrates: 34g; Fiber: 1g; Protein: 5g; Sodium: 292mg; Iron: 2mg*

SEITAN

MAKES ABOUT 1 POUND / PREP TIME: 15 MINUTES, PLUS KNEADING AND RESTING TIME /
COOK TIME: 40 MINUTES
LEFTOVER-FRIENDLY • NUT-FREE • PLAN AHEAD

All hail, seitan! Despite the sound of its name, seitan isn't the food of choice for nefarious vegans. It's a meat substitute made from vital wheat gluten—the main protein of wheat, minus all the starch. Legend says that seitan was invented in ancient China by vegan Buddhist monks. Most people cook their seitan by simmering it, but I prefer to bake it for a heartier texture.

Vegetable oil, for preparing the baking dish
1¼ cups vital wheat gluten
2 tablespoons nutritional yeast
1 tablespoon garlic powder
1 tablespoon onion powder
1 cup vegetable stock, plus more as needed
2 tablespoons low-sodium soy sauce, or tamari
1 tablespoon tomato paste

1. Preheat the oven to 350°F. Lightly coat a small baking dish with vegetable oil, or line it with parchment paper. Set aside.

2. In a large bowl, combine the vital wheat gluten, nutritional yeast, garlic powder, and onion powder.

3. Add the vegetable stock, soy sauce, and tomato paste. Mix until a dough forms. If the mixture seems too dry, add more vegetable stock, 1 tablespoon at a time. Knead the dough for 3 to 5 minutes, or until it becomes elastic. Cover the dough and let it sit for about 15 minutes, then knead it again a few more minutes. The longer you knead the dough, the chewier it will be. Flatten the dough until it's about 1 inch thick and place it in the prepared baking dish.

4. Bake for 20 minutes, flip the seitan, and bake for 20 minutes more. It should be firm and meaty in texture. If it seems too soft, bake for a few more minutes.

5. Slice or chop the cooked seitan and use in your favorite recipe.

6. Refrigerate in an airtight container for up to 6 days, or freeze for up to 6 months.

First-Timer tip: Simmered seitan has a softer texture. If you'd prefer to simmer it, separate the dough into 3 or 4 smaller pieces and gently stretch and flatten each piece. Place the pieces in a large pot with enough vegetable stock to cover them (about 4 cups) and bring the mixture to a boil over medium-high heat. As soon as the liquid begins to boil, reduce the heat to low and simmer for 40 minutes. Remove the pot from the heat and cool the seitan in the stock. Once the seitan has cooled, remove it from the stock and use it in your favorite recipe.

Variation tip: You can vary the taste of your seitan by adding different seasonings to the stock. Try using poultry seasoning for a chicken-style seitan, seaweed for a seafood-flavored seitan, or a vegan Worcestershire sauce for beefy seitan. You can also include aromatics, such as chopped onion or garlic, to infuse extra flavor.

Per serving (2 ounces): *Calories: 116; Fat: 1g; Carbohydrates: 9g; Fiber: 1g; Protein: 20g; Sodium: 291mg; Iron: 0mg*

RESOURCES

WEBSITES

Barnivore.com
Alcohol can sometimes contain gelatin, egg whites, and other animal-based ingredients that don't show up on the label. Barnivore has a large database of wines, beers, and liquors, and it can tell you whether your drink is vegan.

LeapingBunny.org
Cosmetics, skin care products, and household cleaners often contain animal products, or are tested on animals. Leaping Bunny has a comprehensive list of vegan and cruelty-free products.

RaiseVegan.com
This website is a great resource for families. You'll find information on how to stay vegan through pregnancy, raise healthy vegan kids, get vegan news, and find plant-based recipes.

Vegan.com
This website has pretty much everything you need to go vegan, including a starter guide, answers to frequently asked questions, lists of essential cookbooks, and a comprehensive nutrition guide.

VegNews.com
VegNews is a bimonthly magazine, and their website is a great source for all things going on in the world of veganism—from fashion and beauty to health and wellness.

BOOKS

Artisan Vegan Cheese, Miyoko Schinner, Book Publishing Co., 2012
Many people say they can never go vegan because they wouldn't be able to give up cheese. In this cookbook, Miyoko shows you can have your cheese and eat it, too.

Eating Animals, Jonathan Safran Foer, Back Bay Books, 2010
This book is part memoir, part investigative report. It explores the morality of what we eat, and looks at the factory farming system.

How Not to Die: Discover the Foods Scientifically Proven to Prevent and Reverse Disease, Michael Greger, MD, with Gene Stone, Flatiron Books, 2015
In this book, Greger looks at the 15 most common causes of death in America and explains how nutrition and lifestyle changes can help prevent and reverse them.

Living the Farm Sanctuary Life: The Ultimate Guide to Eating Mindfully, Living Longer, and Feeling Better Every Day, Gene Baur with Gene Stone, Rodale Books, 2015
Gene Baur co-founded Farm Sanctuary in 1986, and he shares the basic tenets of Farm Sanctuary living in this book, such as eating in harmony with your values and connecting to nature whenever you can.

Main Street Vegan: Everything You Need to Know to Eat Healthfully and Live Compassionately in the Real World, Victoria Moran and Adair Moran, TarcherPerigee, 2012
This is a practical guide to going vegan, with advice on handling everything from eating out and hosting dinner parties to buying cruelty-free cosmetics and household products.

Sweet Vegan Treats: 90 Recipes for Cookies, Brownies, Cakes, and Tarts, Hannah Kaminsky, Skyhorse, 2019
One of the books that helped me learn how to bake without eggs and butter was Hannah's 2007 book *My Sweet Vegan*. *Sweet Vegan Treats* is a revised and updated version.

The Joyful Vegan: How to Stay Vegan in a World That Wants You to Eat Meat, Dairy, and Eggs, Colleen Patrick-Goudreau, BenBella Books, 2019
For most of us, being vegan goes against social and cultural norms, making it a tough choice to stick with. Colleen shares her wisdom for staying vegan in an omnivore world.

Vegan Chocolate: Unapologetic Luscious and Decadent Dairy-Free Desserts, Fran Costigan, Running Press Adult, 2013
If you're a chocoholic like me, this cookbook will help satisfy all your cravings with the most decadently indulgent vegan desserts.

Veganize It!: Easy DIY Recipes for a Plant-Based Kitchen, Robin Robertson, Houghton Mifflin Harcourt, 2017

Robin shows just how easy it is to make your own vegan staples, including dairy-free milks and cheeses, meatless burgers and sausages, and even butter, in this helpful cookbook.

Why We Love Dogs, Eat Pigs, and Wear Cows: An Introduction to Carnism, Melanie Joy, Red Wheel, 2011

I remember asking my mom why it was okay to eat cows but not cats when I was little. The answer was, "That's just the way it is." This book examines that belief and the way we tend to disconnect our love for animals when it comes to food.

APPS

Bunny Free
Available for Apple and Android
This app helps you check whether skin care, cosmetics, and household products are made without animal products or animal testing.

Happy Cow
Available for Apple and Android
Find vegan and vegan-friendly restaurants and health food stores with this handy app. It includes maps, making it easy to find the nearest veg meal.

Is It Vegan?
Available for Apple and Android
This app enables you to scan the barcode of a product while shopping and find out if it's vegan or not.

Vegaholic
Available for Apple
Vegaholic is a vegan alcohol guide with a comprehensive list of vegan wines, beers, and liquors.

VeGuide
Available for Apple and Android
This app has everything you need to transition to a vegan lifestyle. It includes short daily videos, a progress tracker, and daily quizzes.

DOCUMENTARIES

A Prayer for Compassion, Thomas Wade Jackson, 2019
This film examines the spiritual side of veganism and encourages those on a religious path to expand their circle of compassion to embrace all life, regardless of species. Watch it on Vimeo.

Cowspiracy: The Sustainability Secret, Kip Andersen and Keegan Kuhn, 2014
This film tackles the environmental side of veganism, showing the impact of animal agriculture on the planet. Watch it on Netflix or cowspiracy.com.

Forks Over Knives, Lee Fulkerson, 2011
If you're interested in learning more about how a vegan diet affects your health, this is the film for you. It examines the idea of food as medicine and delves into the scientific research behind the claims that a plant-based diet can prevent many chronic diseases. Watch it on Netflix or forksoverknives.com.

Speciesism: The Movie, Mark Devries, 2013
Speciesism looks at the intellectual side of eating animals, looking for the answer to the question, "Are other species as important as humans?" Watch it on Amazon Prime and Vimeo.

The Game Changers, Louie Psihoyos, 2018
Eating a vegan diet is often seen as kind of a girly thing, because "real men need meat." Featuring interviews with record-winning vegan athletes, this film squashes that stereotype. Watch it on Netflix, iTunes, Google Play, Vimeo, Vudu, and YouTube.

Vegucated, Marisa Miller Wolfson, 2011
In *Vegucated*, three meat- and cheese-loving New Yorkers agree to go vegan for six weeks. The film follows the struggles they face with the new diet as well as their discovery of what exactly goes on in factory farms. Watch it on Amazon Prime and YouTube.

REFERENCES

Friedman, Lisa, Kendra Pierre-Lewis, and Somini Sengupta. "The Meat Question by the Numbers." *New York Times.* January 25, 2018. www.nytimes.com/2018/01/25/climate/cows-global-warming.html.

Greger, Michael, MD, with Gene Stone. *How Not to Die: Discover the Foods Scientifically Proven to Prevent and Reverse Disease.* New York: Flatiron Books, 2015.

Hester, Kathy. *The Great Vegan Beans Book: More than 100 Delicious Plant-Based Dishes Packed with the Kindest Protein in Town!* Beverly, MA: Fair Winds Press, 2013.

Murry, Michael, Joseph Pizzorno, and Lara Pizzorno. *The Encyclopedia of Healing Foods.* New York: Atria Books, 2005.

Steen, Celine, and Tamasin Noyes. *The Great Vegan Grains Book: Celebrate Whole Grains with More than 100 Delicious Plant-Based Recipes.* Beverly, MA: Fair Winds Press, 2015.

INDEX

ACKNOWLEDGMENTS

I couldn't have written this book without the support of Dennis Mason, who washed many, many dishes and taste-tested all the recipes with me.

I owe a huge debt of gratitude to my recipe testers: Beth Bahret, Sarah Eastin, Karyn Gost, Rhonda Jones, Donna M. Kaminski, Paulina Kaminski, Christine Kaminski Brozyniak, Susan Landaira, Eileen Mallor, Connie Maschan, Ruth Schlomer, and Mike Sojkowski. I couldn't have created all these recipes without their help.

A big thank you to my friends and family for their support. I'm eternally grateful to all my vegan blogger friends for their support and encouragement.

And most importantly, thank you so much to the team at Callisto Media, especially Reina Glenn, for entrusting me with this project.

ABOUT THE AUTHOR

 **Dianne Wenz** is a certified holistic health coach, vegan lifestyle coach, and plant-based chef, with a certificate in plant-based nutrition. Dianne coaches people from across the globe, supporting them in improving their health and well-being, as well as making the dietary and lifestyle changes needed to go vegan. She also teaches both private and public cooking classes in the northern New Jersey area. She is the author of *The Truly Healthy Vegan Cookbook*.

Dianne lives in New Jersey with her partner, Dennis Mason, and their cats, Archie, Clementine, Tallulah Belle, and Rupert.

Visit DiannesVeganKitchen.com for healthy living tips, nutrition information, and recipes.